INTRODUCING
Baudrillard

Chris Horrocks and Zoran Jevtic

Edited by Richard Appignanesi

ICON BOOKS UK   TOTEM BOOKS USA

This edition published in the UK
in 1999 by Icon Books Ltd.,
Grange Road, Duxford,
Cambridge CB2 4QF
email: icon@mistral.co.uk
www.iconbooks.co.uk

Distributed in the UK, Europe,
Canada, South Africa and Asia by the
Penguin Group: Penguin Books Ltd.,
27 Wrights Lane, London W8 5TZ

This edition published in Australia
in 1999 by Allen & Unwin Pty. Ltd.,
PO Box 8500, 9 Atchison Street,
St. Leonards NSW 2065

Previously published in the UK and
Australia in 1996 under the title
Baudrillard for Beginners

Reprinted 1997

First published in the United States
in 1996 by Totem Books
Inquiries to: PO Box 223,
Canal Street Station,
New York, NY 10013

Reprinted 1997

In the United States,
distributed to the trade by
National Book Network Inc.,
4720 Boston Way, Lanham,
Maryland 20706

Library of Congress Catalog
Card Number: 96–060483

Text copyright © 1996 Chris Horrocks
Illustrations copyright © 1996 Zoran Jevtic

The author and artist have asserted their moral rights.

Originating editor: Richard Appignanesi

No part of this book may be reproduced in any form, or by any means,
without prior permission in writing from the publisher.

Printed and bound in Australia
by McPherson's Printing Group, Victoria

Jean Baudrillard – Con? Icon? Iconoclast?

As the Marxist critic Douglas Kellner said,
"The whole Baudrillard affair is rapidly mutating into a new idolatry of a new master thinker, and is in danger of giving rise to a new orthodoxy".

Jean Baudrillard's enormous output on mass consumption, media and society stretches from the political turbulence of 1960s France to the global vertigo of the 1990s.

His theoretical position has radically altered over this time...

...from early Marxist critiques of modern consumer culture and society, through a succession of skirmishes with **psychoanalysis, sociology, semiology** and **Marxism** itself, to his rejection of theory and its replacement with an extreme "fatal" vision of the world.

Baudrillard is a contradictory character. The "real" Baudrillard is elusive — almost secretive. In seminars he seems passive and uncertain. Yet the "virtual" Baudrillard is ferociously uncompromising — and his virulent style is met with equal force by critics who accuse him of intolerance, banality, generalization and facetiousness.

It's not just his style they find irksome.

Baudrillard disturbs the theoretical foundations of academia, and intellectuals are wary of his popularity with the media. Academia questions his status as a "serious" intellectual.

So who is Jean Baudrillard —and what has he done to upset people?

I don't think of myself as a philosopher. . . . perhaps a moralist, but certainly not a sociologist.

Although he taught sociology up till the mid 1980s, it's misleading to call him a sociologist — much of his work is intent on destroying the discipline.

It's safe to call Baudrillard a "critical theorist" for his Marxist period and "fatal theorist" later on when his writing style sends theory beyond its limits.

I'm an aeronautical missionary.

BAUDRILLARD

Fasten your seatbelts . . .

I was born in Rheims, France in 1929, just after the "first great crisis of modernity" — the Wall Street Crash.

His grandparents were peasants and his parents civil servants.

The young Jean studied hard at the Lycée, then taught German before taking up sociology. He went to university late, as an assistant at Nanterre, Paris. In 1966, he completed his thesis in sociology.

His interest in politics came with the left's opposition to the Algerian War and his association with Existentialist Jean Paul Sartre's (1905-80) journal *Les Temps Modernes* in 1962-63, for which he wrote literary reviews.

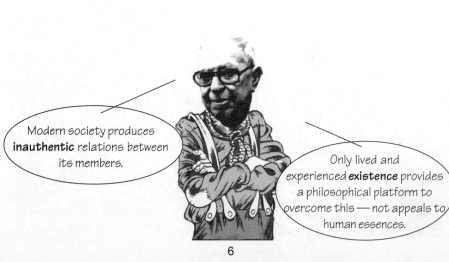

Modern society produces **inauthentic** relations between its members.

Only lived and experienced **existence** provides a philosophical platform to overcome this — not appeals to human essences.

But did Baudrillard adopt my existentialist philosophy?

No, he sided with Henri Lefebvre, the Marxist sociologist.

Sartre's novels are quite simply boring. His philosophy turns human anguish into a mystery overcome by a superhuman moment.

That's inhuman. Anguish is everyday fear and misery. We must reverse this slide into contempt for man and not condemn his triviality.

Lefebvre

Lefebvre's *Critique of Everyday Life* (1958) examined social structures **beyond** the workplace but with an emphasis on Marx's concept of alienation.

Baudrillard did follow Sartre's creation of the "intellectual" as independent from political parties, "free" to build a dialogue with Marxism.

Mass Consumption

In the 1960s, Baudrillard and his contemporaries saw a new France emerging: modernization, technological development, monopoly capitalism and a developing information society of **mass consumption.**

But could traditional Marxism account for or incorporate these upheavals? Was capitalism extending itself beyond the workplace or was this a radical departure?

Identify contradictions between classes in relations of **production** by economic analysis of the commodity?

No, Marx's theories of the mode of production have stalled. Consumption — not production — is the basis of the social order.

Baudrillard's first major project was to provide a critical account for the emergence and effect of **mass consumption**.

Structuralism

But what methodology could he use?
Fashionable **Structuralism** — a method which emphasizes "deep" permanent structures of languages and cultures, which contends that the "subject" is not derived from existence but from language.

I am against structuralism — a system intent on classifying culture is repressive.

No...
I see a structural system at work in consumption — and structuralism could be used to expose its dynamics.

What's the noise?

From May to June 1968, theoretical crisis was eclipsed by social revolt.

MAI 68
DÉBUT D'UNE LUTTE PROLONGÉ

Mon Dieu!

Paris was in riot. In France, 10 million people went on strike. Non-violent marches became pitched battles — the tools were barricades, burning cars and Molotov cocktails. Even Baudrillard's faculty was disrupted for two months.

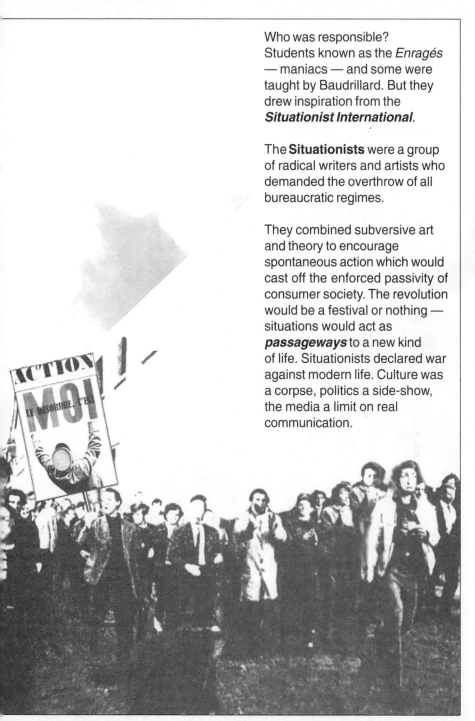

Who was responsible?
Students known as the *Enragés*
— maniacs — and some were
taught by Baudrillard. But they
drew inspiration from the
Situationist International.

The **Situationists** were a group
of radical writers and artists who
demanded the overthrow of all
bureaucratic regimes.

They combined subversive art
and theory to encourage
spontaneous action which would
cast off the enforced passivity of
consumer society. The revolution
would be a festival or nothing —
situations would act as
passageways to a new kind
of life. Situationists declared war
against modern life. Culture was
a corpse, politics a side-show,
the media a limit on real
communication.

Capital accumulates until it becomes image. TV, football matches, art galleries, traffic... The spectacle is not a collection of images *but a social relationship among people, mediated by images.*

Repressive Participation

Jean was not a member and was pessimistic about the effectiveness of an uprising which quickly turned into news footage.

The revolution failed. Some historians think it expired because the students went on summer holiday.

This May 1968 revolt was "hare-brained". Students had thought that capitalist repression meant aggression, but in fact it *encouraged* **participation**.

Baudrillard called this new form of repression **ambience** — where society becomes controlled through its inclusion in the spectacle of consumption.

Baudrillard had contempt for the repressive code of consumption. It was not just a passive moment after goods were produced and sold but a new phase of capitalism... **affluent society**.

Affluent Society

Affluent society "mutates" the human species.
We are no longer surrounded by people but by objects. This is the new consumer ambience — a new morality which systematically structures modern life, and where unique relations between an object, a place and function have disappeared.

This liberation of **objects** from life gives us an ambient experience of diffuseness and mobility — smoking, reading, entertaining, air tickets, credit cards, movies, gourmet shops, clothing are part of ambient connectedness.

£295
£195-
£699-
£850-
£3999
£300-
£3399-

Work, leisure, nature and culture were once separate and produced anxiety and complexity in our real life. Now they're mixed, massaged, climate-controlled and domesticated in the simple activity of **perpetual shopping**.

Sign Network

Department stores and malls magically negate scarcity and synthesize all consumer activities — leisure, spectacle, consumption — offering a **universalist model** which invades all aspects of social life.

Store displays refer the consumer not to the objects' function but to their collective meaning — a **calculus** or **network** of signs.

CREDITS

£20K

£2699-
Real Fake

PAY HERE

Life-size!
£199-
Real plastic

In the ambient order, the consumer object itself is less important than its value in the ambient harmony of consumer signs.

We are immersed in a modern world of signs which destroy tradition. Our experience of plastics, synthetics, pastel colours, lighting systems, replace earlier "living" materials like wood, stucco and cotton.

This systematization invades the domestic interior. Take colour. In the 19th century colours had no independent value from the particular objects they expressed - their symbolic meanings always arrived from their context.

In the early 20th century, colours became **liberated** and separated from forms. They had a life of their own. Anything could be red, or blue, or green.
Later there is a backlash — and pastel harmonizes the ambient environment — colour disappears as such and we are left with **tonal systems.**

Because many objects have a **functionalist** logic, we become functional.

Right dear?

Multi-purpose products make multi-purpose people.

The Critic as Consumer

Our existence is lived by the rhythm of consumer goods. Objects are stripped of symbolism and expression. In this consumer world everything is "handy" - muscular effort is replaced with **cybernetic**, often remote, control.

His pad in Paris is surrounded by restaurants, cinemas, small shops. Baudrillard usually wears brown, smokes Gauloises roll-ups (peasant background?).
The apartment is unpretentious, with plain drapes over the furniture, black and white photos on the wall, a mirror over the fireplace, a TV, video recorder and CD. He has a second home in Languedoc and two children.

Defining the Ambient Consumer

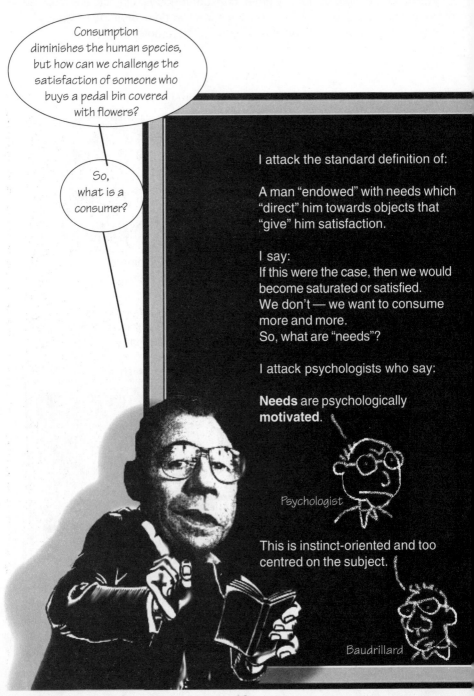

Need is explained by social dynamics such as conformity and competition — needs are learnt.

Sociologist

Sociology gets us nowhere. It is a tautology: "An individual belongs to a particular group which consumes a particular product. The individual consumes such a product because he belongs to such a group..." etc.

Baudrillard

Needs are embedded in consumer goods, and desires are manipulated by the arrangement of goods. Needs are rational.

Economist

"So, needs above the socially desirable are false needs. It is the mark of an enfeebled imagination to suggest that two automobiles to a family is sufficient."

John Kenneth Galbraith, economist (1908)

No! We can't cast off this apparent "conditioning" and limit our needs to "real" ones — it is impossible to know which are real needs and which are not.

Besides, **consumers never feel mystified or alienated**. We "play" with needs, substituting one object for another.

Individual **choice** is the ideology of the industrial system. Freedom of choice is **imposed** on the consumer.

Baudrillard's conclusion is that individually **needs are nothing**. Needs have nothing to do with any correspondence between a consumer and an object. **The system of needs is produced by the system of production.**

Applying Semiology

This woolly definition of needs and consumers was refined when Baudrillard introduced his structural logic of consumption, where he suggested that the consumer was an *effect* of the way that consumer goods circulate as meanings — forget the consumer.

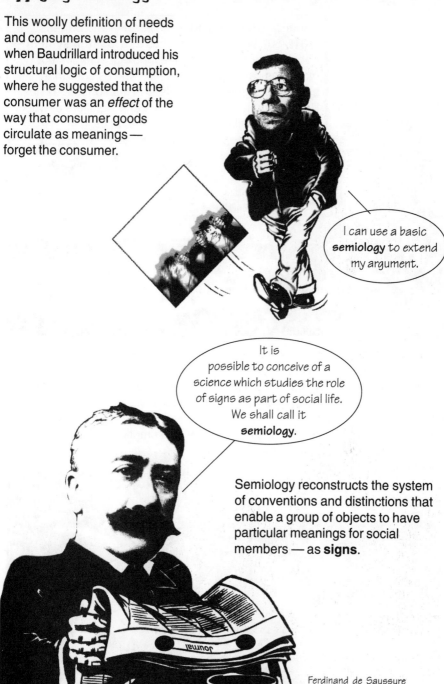

I can use a basic **semiology** to extend my argument.

It is possible to conceive of a science which studies the role of signs as part of social life. We shall call it **semiology**.

Semiology reconstructs the system of conventions and distinctions that enable a group of objects to have particular meanings for social members — as **signs**.

Ferdinand de Saussure (1857-1913) — founder of structural linguistics.

Baudrillard followed his associate, Roland Barthes (1915-80), who studied clothes as a **fashion system** — not simply the outcome of technological forces but mainly as carriers of information and as units in a system of **signs** — particularly in fashion magazines. Barthes analyses the signifieds and signifiers at work in sentences like: *prints win at the races.*

A sign =
signifier - an image, sound, word: prints
signified- its concept, meaning: races

Consumption is like a linguistic system (*langue*) — the relation of fashion objects/signs to each other (coats to jackets) — in opposition to individual effects of speech (*parole*) — the innumerable uses of clothes as signs by individuals and groups.

Baudrillard emphasizes the abstract **code** of consumption, which organizes and differentiates objects as signs, rather than individual expressions of need and pleasure in or for the object.

Classifying Consumers

Baudrillard says: "Consumption, in so far as it is meaningful, is a systematic act of the manipulation of signs. Objects are categories of objects which quite tyrannically induce categories of persons."

We don't just consume objects as signs — we consume **relations between objects**. This is a recent cultural development.

Social difference is organized by the **system of objects**.

Once upon a time there were Chippendale tables and farm tables.

If you weren't noble you couldn't buy into the **style** of the former.

Today though, no **class** chasm separates them. They are part of the same **system** of **objects** into which **all** consumers are inserted.

£2700- Chippendale

Sign Function of Objects

The relational differences in quality and cultural value of an object system classify consumers.

Anyone who has bought a fake walnut bedroom set to realize a dream of social promotion knows that superior "harmonious" (i.e. genuine) interiors exist in the market place.

The series (mass-produced) table is a stereotype of the model (original/unique) table. It is flimsy, made of cheaper, imitative materials.

I experience the latter as models from which I am separated not by class but by lack of money.

He is enmeshed in an oppressive structure of signification — meanings generated from the differential relation of signs.

An object is not an object of consumption unless it is liberated as a **sign** caught up in the circulation of such differences.

Baudrillard's selective use of semiology foregrounds the **sign function** of the object. This is what makes objects circulate as meanings.

Denotation and Connotation

The fridge **denotes** its use/object: preserving or freezing food.	The fridge **connotes** or "plays" as element of comfort, prestige, or even "functionalism".

Objects cannot interchange their direct function with others. (A fridge doesn't make toast.) Outside this **denotative** function, objects can be **substituted** with each other virtually infinitely — in the field of **connotation** — where the objects become interchangeable and circulated as signs (of status, wealth, "good design" etc.)

This signifying "play" **is** consumption. All objects could be substituted for the fridge at this level — as all could be signs of prestige and so on.

Our needs and choices **hysterically** follow this unlimited interchangeability of signs — and not the particular function of the object.

If we acknowledge that a need is not a need for a particular object as much as it is a "need" for difference (**the desire for social meaning**), only then will we understand that satisfaction can never be fulfilled, and consequently

Crazy Consumers?

So what does the consumer desire — if he is not satisfied with signs of consumption?

Baudrillard attempts to foreground the pathological nature of consumption by hijacking psychoanalysis.

A neurotic illness — obsession — results when the frustrated adult regresses to the phase in his childhood where early libidinal development was disturbed.

Sigmund Freud (1856-1939)

Yes, the **collector**. He regresses to the anal phase — expressed by accumulation and retention. His passion is not for **possessing** objects themselves but stems from his fanaticism for an illusory wholeness — for completing the set. But really he is trying to re-collect himself!

And if he gets the last object in the collection, he is effectively signifying his own death . . .

But doesn't this mean that my "subjective" desire is subversive of the system of objects and signification?

No. Objects **absorb** cultural anxiety (about the loss of the past etc.) and allow regression, but it is expressed **in the system** of cultural consumption: "what man lacks is always invested in the object."

Today taboos and neuroses don't make the individual a deviant or an outlaw.

Individual repression has been annulled because it's found a home in objects. But the social organization of objects brings its own repression.

Consumer freedom means freedom to regress and be irrational!

Regressing with Consumer Objects

With which objects?

Bygones: Signify time and past. A desperate narcissistic attempt to regress to childhood and to find Mother (origins) and Father (authenticity).

Household Pets? Indicate failure of human relationships and narcissism. Neutered, they regulate castration anxiety.

Wrist-watches? Absorb anguish of death.

Why isn't pleasure the basis of consumption?

Because pleasure is not about enjoyment — it's about duty. It springs not from the individual but from social obligation. The consumer must strive for happiness and pleasure.

It's the inverse of the wise and thrifty Puritan ethic which demands financial restraint.

So what's this new ethic called?

The Fun System

With "fun morality" the consumer must not be passive. He must try everything.

> Try Jesus, Jacko's new album, love — Japanese style!

If he becomes satisfied with what he has, he becomes asocial — and not part of the system of consumption.

So what sort of consumer object is it that constantly dissatisfies him?

A myth. We must treat the object as **nothing** but types of relations and significations — and look at the hidden (unconscious) **logic** which arranges these relations.

30

Logic of the Consumer Object

Baudrillard's logic of the consumer object updates Marx's conception of a commodity as use value (its utility) and economic exchange value (its price). The object of consumption today consists of:

1. A **functional** logic of **use value** — e.g. a hammer which hits nails (an instrument).

2. An **economic** logic of **exchange value** — e.g. it can be exchanged for something else or money (as a commodity).

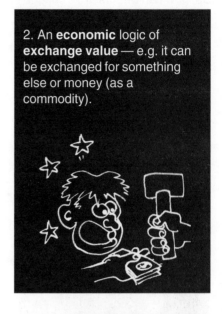

3. A logic of **symbolic exchange** — e.g. a wedding ring, unique to two people, reciprocated, ambivalent, symbolizing an occasion, place and time.

4. A logic of **sign exchange value** — e.g. an ordinary ring I wear as a sign for others, substitutable and a part of the fashion system (a sign).

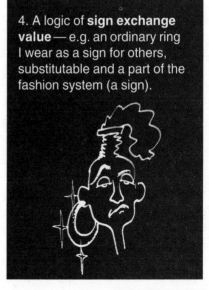

Symbolic exchange is crucial to Baudrillard.

Symbolic Exchange

Happy now? Yes, the logic that organizes these objects is ultimately the system of consumption, which is determined by the system of production.

But how can Baudrillard's critique evade this all-encompassing system? What kind of world is he defending?

Baudrillard's whole critique is launched from the platform of **symbolic exchange.**

He draws from anthropologist **Marcel Mauss's** (1872-1950) theorization of the **gift**. What is given and returned is not necessarily a physical present, reflecting wealth, or property. It can consist of courtesies, rituals, women, dances, the recognitions of status. In primitive society, a gift has to be repaid because the recipient is under social obligation to do so — and failure to do so equals social censure. The elements of gift-exchange are related to individuals and groups and not just objects.

Symbolic exchange is therefore radically opposed to the abstraction of economic and sign exchange. It is open-ended and it doesn't **accumulate** meanings (or profits) or alienate, because it doesn't split people from their identity or their social place by inserting them into the system of objects.

It wasn't long before Baudrillard saw that semiology itself was not a way of demythologizing the consumer world — **it was part of the problem**. Structural linguistics and semiology **were** capitalism.

This manipulation, that plays on the faculty of producing **meaning** and difference, is more radical than that which plays on labour power.

Are there structural similarities between the commodity form — which allows goods to circulate in the way Marx had claimed — and the **sign form** which **allows meanings to circulate**?

Is there a **political economy of the sign**?

By the way, you wouldn't know who wrote on our menu board?

Coke

The Innocence of Use Value

Marx uses the famous example of Daniel Defoe's **Robinson Crusoe** to show that the mystical character of commodities does **not** originate in their use value.

So far as a commodity has a value in use, there is nothing mysterious about it. Man changes the forms of the materials furnished by nature in such a way as to make them useful to him.

Goods **only** have use values for him, under the sign of Nature.

Marx is claiming that a product is useful before anything else. Economic exchange harms social relations (profit = exploitation) and innocent old use value gives the commodity a "humanity".

Marx has fallen into a trap. By opposing commodity value to the simple, "transparent" relation of Crusoe to his modest wealth, Marx only underlined the bourgeois **myth of primary needs**, which also champions individual autonomy, man as non-alienated labour and a moral consciousness bound to nature.

Use value is born of economics — it does not exist beforehand. It is the ideology of capitalism.

Besides, what on earth is Man Friday doing there?

You rang, master?

5 o'clock... I could use a drink!

The Mask of "Use Value"

Baudrillard's radicality lies in this statement: the utility of objects is **not** a property **prior** to exchange value.
Use value is an effect of exchange value. It is an **alibi** which keeps products circulating. **Use value props up exchange value**. It is produced as a **sign** rather than a fundamental truth.

Use value is not outside the system — it only integrates us more effectively into the system!

When we call goods "useful", we are making their use value the first and last reason for their existence. Worse, we turn all objects into an abstract finality: everything is useful!

For Baudrillard, only **symbolic exchange** objects escape this abstraction. Once exchanged, objects are bound up with social obligation. "It is **this** gift and not another". To call it "useful" abstracts it and makes it equivalent to all other objects under the sign of "utility". This is reductive and destructive.

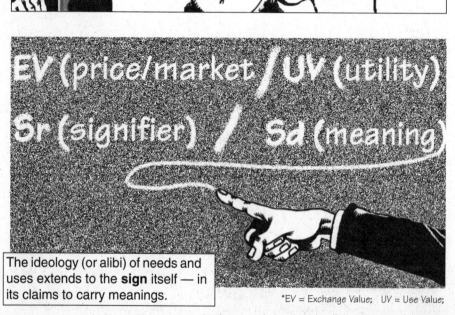

The ideology (or alibi) of needs and uses extends to the **sign** itself — in its claims to carry meanings.

*EV = Exchange Value;   UV = Use Value;

Does Ideology Reflect Reality?

This conjecture was so radical it meant the term "ideology" had to be redefined. Marxist philosophers had thought ideology consisted of representations or signs (like theology, for example) which unconsciously reflected men's productive relation to the world.

Baudrillard suggested that this assumed that ideology was like an after-effect of the mode of production — like a surface of signs on top of economy. He claimed ideology ran deeper than this.

Ideology extends **through the construction of the sign itself** in its claim to present reality or meaning.

So are reality and meaning an alibi to allow signs to circulate?

And do signs refer to an objective meaning and reality?

The Reply of Structural Linguistics

Structural linguistics **assumed that signs can refer to an objective reality** — but in a misconceived way.

Baudrillard now claims that the sign is an accomplice of capital. Why is this?

1. Because it is an agent of abstraction.

2. It universally reduces all potential and qualities of meaning. The meaning is "framed" when a signifier is tied to the signified.

3. It excludes and discriminates. Once installed, a sign offers itself as a full value — positive, rational, exchangeable.

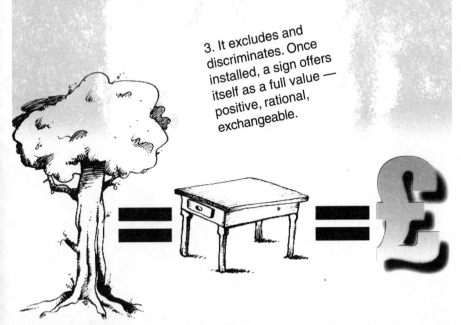

This is the rationality of the sign. Its rationality does NOT lie in the sign **naming** some exterior reality (a tree over there), but in its **exclusion** of ambivalence or non-resolution of meaning.

Is the "Sun" Real?

The signifier (sound-image "sun") refers to a signified (the concept-meaning, "sun") and together they make up a **referent** — THE SUN.

No!
Reality is governed by the sign — projected by it. The "referent" is the reflection of the sign.

The "Sun" as signifier (image or word) restricts and induces its signified (concept) and becomes a sign. The real sun (referent) is an **effect** of this logic.

But where is the "sign-crime" here?

The holiday sun signifies only a **POSITIVE** value — the source of happiness. It is opposed not to itself (as "bad" sun) — which would make the sign ambivalent and destructive of meaning — but to its constructed opposite: non - sun (rain).

Symbolic exchange loses out. Our sun is not **symbolic** of life and death, goodness and vengeance, as it was for Aztecs or Ancient Egyptian cultures. It has no **destructive power or ambivalence**.

And so **reality is in collusion with the sign**. It is a reality-effect produced by the sign. The sign alludes to reality, but in actuality excludes it.

The real sun does not exist! This is the **semiological reduction**.

For Baudrillard, this capitalist "control" of meaning and reality is terroristic.

Symbolic exchange — unique, ambivalent, reciprocated functions of objects or symbols — is flattened. All repressive and **reductive** strategies of power systems are already present in the internal logic of the sign, including political economy.

Déconstruction... against "Presence"

Baudrillard owes a debt to the poststructuralist **Jacques Derrida**.

Derrida questioned the primacy of the **signified** in western rational philosophy — the repressive promotion of the **metaphysics of presence**: the desire for a guarantee of certainty, immediacy, origin or foundation for meaning. Derrida called this radical criticism **déconstruction**.

My **déconstruction** attempts to locate the metaphysical assumptions which any text — philosophy, semiology — hides or represses in order to remain viable.

Similarly, I can say that use-value is the metaphysical opposition to exchange-value, or signified/referent to signifier, or unconscious to conscious . . .

AZTEC
Travel

SUN!

HEAT!

Jacques Derrida (b.1930).

47

Nowhere do signs carve out and organize reality more effectively than in culture.

I have always had a kind of radical suspicion towards culture.

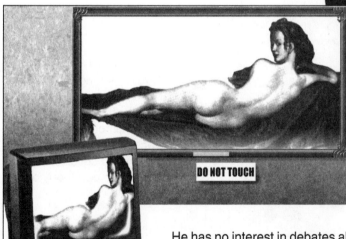

Baudrillard writes of both high culture: "avantgarde" art, design and aesthetics, and mass culture: TV, film, etc.

DO NOT TOUCH

He has no interest in debates about vulgarization (where the content of high culture is seen degraded when produced for a television audience).

Culture is the production and consumption of signs. But because signs carve out reality for us, in effect EVERYTHING IS NOW "CULTURAL", available as image and "meaning".

Simulations

Everything is now Cultural? What does this mean?

Culture is no longer a "living body", the presence of a collectivity (religion, feasts, storytelling) producing signs. Now signs **produce** cultures.

Baudrillard is insisting that culture should involve a symbolic function (surprise!). It should be open to argument, reciprocal exchange, and didactic process. It should comment on and criticize itself and so upset the ceremony of mass culture.

Culture is described by dynamics of **consumption** — fashion cycles, ambience, codes. No aspect of culture escapes this.

The main example of this is cultural recycling — ephemeral signs of past culture which are produced as **simulations**.

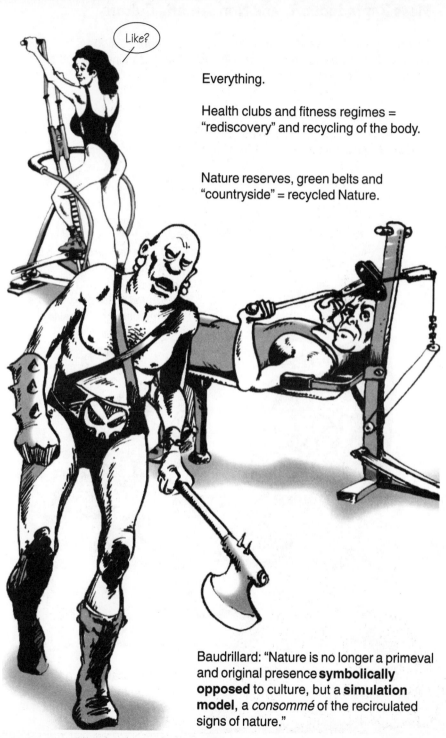

Everything.

Health clubs and fitness regimes = "rediscovery" and recycling of the body.

Nature reserves, green belts and "countryside" = recycled Nature.

Baudrillard: "Nature is no longer a primeval and original presence **symbolically opposed** to culture, but a **simulation model**, a *consommé* of the recirculated signs of nature."

51

Mass Reproduction... and Non-Auratic Culture

Technologies of **mass reproduction** produce culture as signs.
The problem here is of the original work of art and its infinite reproduction through mass media.

That which withers in the age of **mechanical reproduction** is the **aura** of the work of art. The technique of reproduction detaches the reproduced object from the domain of tradition and substitutes a plurality of copies for a unique existence.

But it's no good blaming industry or society for spreading this type of **non-auratic** culture. Van Gogh's significance is not tied to **mass-reproduction** itself but springs from sign exchange —Van Gogh-as-sign circulated in the cycle of fashion — the **code**. Its manufacture by machines is beside the point.

Walter Benjamin (1892-1940)

SALE

Van Gogh is "sold" as a meaning in the same ephemeral system which imposes itself on high-street clothes or TV programming. Thus, the code organizes "Van Gogh" as cultural form and its meaning stems from it. Van Gogh for sale as a sign!

Lowest Common Culture

"Culture today is misunderstood", said Baudrillard. He called it LCC — Lowest Common Culture. It's not about acquiring culture as knowledge, but about participation and integration in questions and answers: for instance, quiz shows, quiz games — even school exams.

Like who? The **Frankfurt School of Marxism** sought to take account of the centrality of mass communication in modern societies. The **culture industry** supplies ideologies and mediates experience. **Technology** is its medium — it leads to an **insane** rationality.

The Frankfurt School vs. Mass Culture

The progressive aim of the 18th century Enlightenment has produced its opposite — progress has turned into tyranny. It subordinates the natural world to **technical control** and produces **pseudo-individuality.** Here are two voices from the Frankfurt School...

Theodor Adorno (1903-69) claimed that the **dialectic** (or internal form) of Arnold Schoenberg's (1874-1951) **atonal music** revealed and **contradicted** the tyrannical harmony of bourgeois musical naturalness. But later he saw no hope for a critical culture.

To write poetry after Auschwitz is barbaric. And I hate jazz.

Herbert Marcuse (1898-1979): "Today's novel feature is the flattening out of the antagonism between culture and social reality through the obliteration of the oppositional, alien, and transcendent elements in the higher culture by virtue of which it constituted another dimension of reality."

I call this — **one-dimensional society.**

Herbie

Like the sign system of objects, the signs of culture integrate everyone.

So is Baudrillard critical of **high** culture or of **mass** culture?

Both. All aspects of culture are ephemeral signs. They are not produced to last, except as an ideal or metaphysical reference — like "Nature", after it has been destroyed.

Why? Because high and mass culture are both organized by the code of consumption — the fashion cycle.

Cultural prizes — like the Tate Gallery's Turner Prize — are awarded to one artist per year and are adapted to the functional cycle of modern culture. Once such a prize would have meant the art was reserved for posterity. Now it's singled it out as the latest trend.

The Techno Culture...

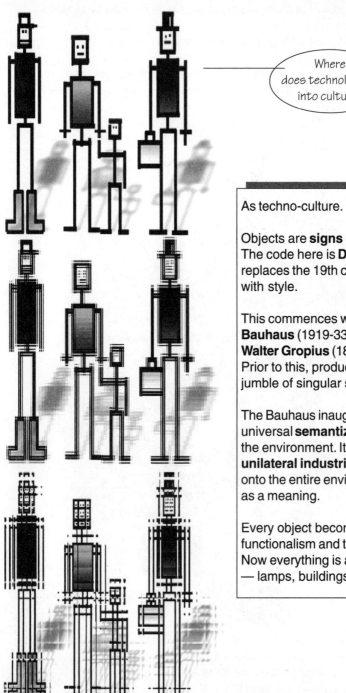

Where does technology fit into culture?

As techno-culture.

Objects are **signs** of technology. The code here is **DESIGN,** which replaces the 19th century concern with style.

This commences with the German **Bauhaus** (1919-33), directed by **Walter Gropius** (1883-1969). Prior to this, products were a jumble of singular styles.

The Bauhaus inaugurated the universal **semantization** of the environment. It projected a **unilateral industrial aesthetic** onto the entire environment as a meaning.

Every object becomes a sign of functionalism and technology. Now everything is a design object — lamps, buildings, cities, people...

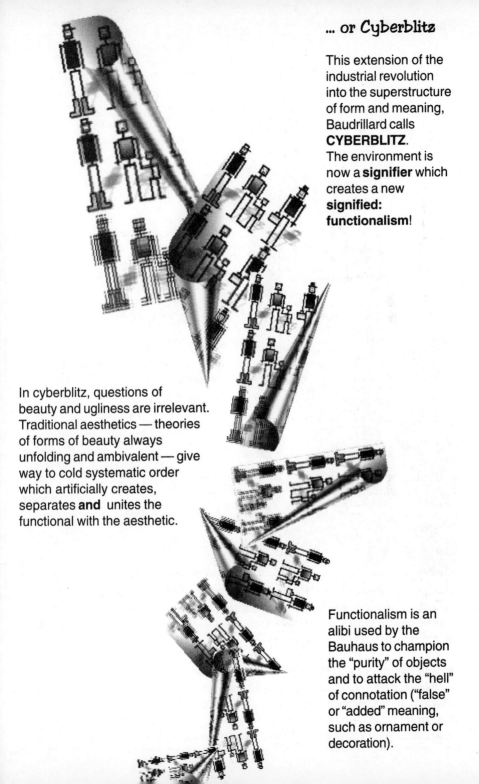

... or Cyberblitz

This extension of the industrial revolution into the superstructure of form and meaning, Baudrillard calls **CYBERBLITZ**. The environment is now a **signifier** which creates a new **signified: functionalism**!

In cyberblitz, questions of beauty and ugliness are irrelevant. Traditional aesthetics — theories of forms of beauty always unfolding and ambivalent — give way to cold systematic order which artificially creates, separates **and** unites the functional with the aesthetic.

Functionalism is an alibi used by the Bauhaus to champion the "purity" of objects and to attack the "hell" of connotation ("false" or "added" meaning, such as ornament or decoration).

Decoration is again simply another **alibi** to prop up the Bauhaus "truth" of functionalist objects. It disguises the fact that there is no absolutely utilitarian object.

It is only an after-effect of the nuanced differences between functionalist objects. They only really "function" as signs of function. And, of course, functionalism enters the code of fashion as just one sign amongst others — postmodern, kitsch, retro . . .

Kitsch? Another pseudo-object. Trashy simulations and overworking of signs — like clichés in language. They exist not because of people's bad taste or manufacturers' profit motive. They are tied to social mobility — part of a hierarchy which separates the abundance of kitsch from the restricted number of high-class goods. They are signs in a code of social distinction.

And Gadgets?

Same logic. They're seen as useless objects (a five-speed toothbrush), but in fact they have a purpose — as a distinctive sign whose signified is technology. Gadgets are like games. They play with the **idea** of function (by adding more knobs or functions), but like all design they are caught in the codes of fashion and sign exchange.

Signs of design circulate everywhere: designer bodies and sex, designer drugs, designer politics. The culture of design replaces reality — its code is triumphant.

Is there no escape from the sign? What about art — doesn't that evade the code?

I have an allergy to culture with a big C — the ideology of the culture of art. I'm a peasant at heart.

Baudrillard admires art for its struggle to represent the object — but not as a practice.

Ironically, his ideas have had their greatest influence in fine art, particularly in New York. The "reluctant prophet" delivered the grim message that art is finished — it's simply a consumption of signs.

Art was initially a sign of **prestige**.

The art market and its sign exchange value does not stem from economic profits or **accumulation**. It comes from exhibiting signs of **expenditure**.

The American social theorist **Thorstein Veblen** (1857-1929) thought that the capitalist profit motive meant that **consumption** was determined by production of useless goods, culminating in the desire of the **leisure class** to challenge, emulate and impress others by **conspicuous** wasteful signs of wealth signifying economic expenditure, or by inconspicuous consumption when the lower classes started to consume conspicuously.

Baudrillard's reaction: "Today it's not just about buying signs of power, it's about controlling the code — the process of signification. The elite are not separated from the rabble by purchasing power alone, but by their exclusive and privileged access to signs — and by being at the top end."

Money is not offered for the use-value of the painting. It is **wagered** for sign exchange value. There is no fixed price, and it is more about outbidding than bartering. Art auctions are "sign-wars".

So what is an art lover? A social groupie who exists in relation to the obsessions of all other art lovers with signs of privilege, just as the painting is related to all other paintings of status in reference to its pedigree — who signed it and who possessed it.

The art lover promotes culture as universal value, because he can never own it.

Banking on Galleries

So galleries and museums are like banks — they both circulate signs. Banks guarantee the universality of money. Galleries make paintings "democratically" available. But only the elite can possess either.

So art is just a sign?

Yes, but one which does not refer to a reality. In the past, painted **copies** had value because they took inspiration from an original, transcendent Natural reality or order, not the "original" painting. So the authenticity of art was not an issue. Forgeries did not exist.

What is a "True" Work of Art?

Today, however, the world no longer guarantees the meaning of the painting. Only the unique gesture and signature of the absent artist can do that, no matter how "impersonal".

Now originality is not about the world but the artist and his succession of signs (the oeuvre).

A fake Soulages work throws suspicion on all Soulages, because the authenticity of the sign is then in question. That is why the art world hates forgery.

This is all art is. It tries to represent the world and be authentic, gestural or emotional. Artists are "naive and pious" — the structure of art as sign exchange undermines "avantgarde" attempts to throw pots of paint at the systematized world.

But can art **represent** the world of mass consumption — of systems of objects? No, art has been playing out its own **disappearance** over the last century. It no longer represents — it **simulates**.

Art has always been a discourse on the objects it represents. The status of these objects in art has changed in the 20th century. Art has increasingly abstracted objects from their social space and turned them into signs which no longer refer back to moral, psychological or symbolic values that used to be tied to the social order.

The evolution of Mondrian's "tree".

The Genealogy of Art's Disappearance

With **Cubism**, objects become **autonomous** elements in the analysis of space. As images/signs they are fragmented to the point of abstraction.

> When everything is aesthetic, nothing is beautiful or ugly any more, and art itself disappears.

Then **Dada** and **Surrealism** parodically revived objects to show them as **irrationally** split from modern, functionalist culture. They attempted to revolt against this "reality" of objects, but only perpetuated the elevation of objects to the artistic code.

> Dada "proves" art with **anti**-art.

Abstraction — expressive or geometrical — represents objects in decomposition and expresses the systematization of the rational order, not the world.

And then comes **Pop Art**, which pretends to reconcile images of objects with consumer objects themselves. Images claim to represent the order of consumption in the industrial and serial production of art and the consumer objects.

So can Pop Art Culture **represent** consumer life?

Baudrillard says no, because it's **integrated with it**. Pop Art comes off the same assembly line. It claims to reflect on Americanness-as-ideology. But Pop Art is itself one of its trademarks.

But surely pop artists enjoy this complicity?

Maybe, but they see it at a different level.

Pop artists assume a reality to objects which they "discover" in its everydayness.

A flag was just a flag.

Jasper Johns (b 1930)

There is no essence of the everyday or the commonplace, and so there can be no art of the everyday — there's nothing to represent.

But don't postmodern artists like **Jeff Koons** and **Mark Kostabi** expose and celebrate the loss of authenticity and critical representation, and the triumph of the art as commodity and sign?

Mark Kostabi (b.1964) is shunned by the art world because he pays art students $7 an hour to produce his paintings sold at $20,000 — all signed KOSTABI...

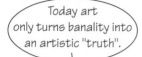

Kostabi ironizes the artist-as-sign by playing the artist-as-creator.

Today art only turns banality into an artistic "truth".

Baudrillard is a total jerk. He doesn't understand America.

Nonetheless Baudrillard is used as a reference by fine artists everywhere. He says they've misunderstood him.

Simulated art... an activity itself nostalgic for the reality of activity in art.

Peter Halley, a simulationist painter of cells and conduits.

I have no response to postmodern art. My writings can justify anything. But to represent them in art is misguided. Painting can never represent simulation because its logic **is** simulation.

In simulation there can be no references or meanings. Artists who reiterate simulation are in a death-like state.

Remarkably silly!
art critic Robert Hughes (b. 1938)

Baudrillard is ultimately ambivalent about art. Art gives a meaning to something which is meaningless. That's its failure and strength. But it might survive by becoming absurdly expensive — as **hyperart**!

The Beaubourg Effect

The **Pompidou Centre** in Paris is attacked by Baudrillard as the worst signifier of modern culture.

The interior tries to present cultural memory (museum), but it looks more like a supermarket. The whole building signifies the disappearance of culture.

The mass public want to challenge sterile culture with its physical destruction. Over 30,000 people inside and the building might fall down! In the Beaubourg the masses don't reflect on culture, but touch, eat and steal it. This cultural violence is about overload and implosion rather than transcendence.

It **deters** culture. Like the monolith in the Sci-Fi film *2001*, it absorbs the energy of its surroundings. It looks like a nuclear power station. It destroys secrecy...

Baudrillard however, is an amateur photographer — and was a contributing editor of *Artforum*.

1973 – Baudrillard Destroys Marxism

Just as culture replaces itself with empty signs which hide its disappearance, capitalism turns into **hypercapitalism** and **signs** of production are mirrored through western society — and beyond.

In 1973, Baudrillard wrote a scathing attack on Marxism. It was responsible for maintaining the **mirror of production** — and exporting it.

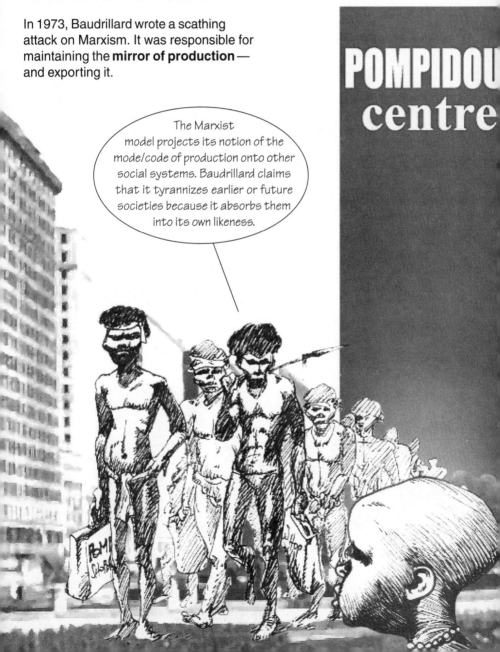

The Marxist model projects its notion of the mode/code of production onto other social systems. Baudrillard claims that it tyrannizes earlier or future societies because it absorbs them into its own likeness.

POMPIDOU
centre

Baudrillard undermines all the Marxian productivist metaphysics in turn...

First, the concept of man as **labour**.

Men begin to distinguish themselves from animals as soon as they begin to produce their means of subsistence.

Labour is a sign which induces the meaning of labour as use/value. This code allows labour to permeate human values.

Production is not just our economic form, it's our form of **representation**. It produces the very conception of labour — power as the fundamental human potential or meaning.

Labour is close to being an **ethic** , even for Marx.

Here Baudrillard follows the sociologist **Max Weber** (1864-1920).

I drew attention to the role of religious thought in shaping economic behaviour, and the nature of modern bureaucratic organization. It's in **Calvinism** that the roots of capitalism are to be found.

The Marxist sign of production extends to the world. "History" equals the history of **the modes of production**. Marxism thus becomes imperialistic. All possible societies have to account for themselves in relation to the productivist model. Thus, traditional societies are seen as non-productivist or **underdeveloped**.

And Psychoanalysis? And Nature?

Even the western rationalist productivist discourse of **psychoanalysis** is caught up in this code. Suddenly, all cultures have a more or less "developed" unconscious, a repressive mechanism.

And **nature** dances to the tune of production...

Labour is grounded in the concept of Nature. Once, Nature signified an order in which men and things were separated.
By the 18th century, Nature becomes a potential power and a myth as it is technologically dominated.
It becomes the great "Referent".
Capitalism is separated from Nature — which is now a sign of production — and it is used as an argument for or against capitalism (bourgeois or Marxist economics).

So Nature is **semiologically reduced** and split into...

Good nature: dominated and a source of wealth.
Bad nature: hostile and polluted.

Like Freud's unconscious, Nature exists as a repressed wealth waiting to be liberated in all its "truth".

This conceptual violence is more destructive than missionaries or venereal disease...

Instead of exporting Marxism and psychoanalysis, we should bring all the force and questioning of primitive societies to bear on Marxism and pyschoanalysis.

In the symbolic order, primitive man does not gauge himself in relation to Nature. Nature is not a value from which he extracts his meaning.

"The Accursed Share"

For Baudrillard, traditional and primitive "societies" do not restrict production of goods. Their symbolic exchange is based on non-production, eventual destruction and a process of unlimited reciprocity between persons, and on limitation of exchanged goods. Production has no meaning.

Baudrillard is drawing on **Georges Bataille's vision of excess** — the "accursed share" which is more fundamental than the accumulative drive of production.

My general economy emphasizes **waste, sacrifice,** and **destruction**.

Even the sun expends energy without asking anything back. And human beings are creatures of excess... Sacrificial economy or symbolic exchange is exclusive of political economy (and of its critique, which is only its completion).

Georges Bataille (1897-1962)

If only anthropologists had seen this, then it would have thrown a radical perspective on our assumptions about art.

Anthropology contributes to a better understanding of objectified thought and its mechanisms. It doesn't matter whose minds we examine, as long as we recognize that cultures' minds display an intelligible structure.

Claude Levi-Strauss (b.1908).

This is the "extreme of liberal thought" which cares for primitives and yet preserves the priority of western thought within this dialogue. Primitive societies don't have a culture. They are lived in the symbolic, not in the sign. They have a society of them and outsiders, we have one of universalized humanity.

The Slave and Wage Worker

Marx projects capitalism onto slavery:

The slave is an exploited labourer.

Slave/master is not economic domination but a reciprocal relation — not between two separate subjects, but in terms of symbolic **obligation**. The salaried labourer's "liberation" is just western humanist rationality conceiving all earlier forms of domination as irrational. We should look at our own society as an exploited one.

But if Marxism is inadequate because it cannot illuminate past structures except as relatively different from capitalism this means that **no** standpoint in the present can study past structures. This is pure relativism.

Lacan's Mirror

Baudrillard thinks it's more like **Lacan's mirror stage**: through the mirror of production, human comes to consciousness in the imagination. He identifies and objectifies himself in his ideal as **productivist ego**.

This sounds like simulated labour.

We no longer "work" in the classic sense — we keep ourselves occupied in the ritual of the **signs** of labour.

Production has mutated into a tyrannical code organizing everything from road building, body building, working on a tan, and retraining. We are not dragged away from daily life to surrender to machines — we are integrated with "flexi-time", "home working" or "unemployment benefit".

Jacques Lacan (b. 1901)

83

Today production doesn't produce consumption, consumption produces signs of production!

Wages can go up or down. Bosses don't worry, as long as the workers hold on to the **meaning** of work.

Unions enter the sign of pay-bargaining. They are the accomplices of workers and bosses — they keep the signs of exploitation and liberation in suspense.

Strikes were once organized violence against violence of capital to extract some surplus value: the workers seizing profits.

Now striking for strike's sake is the absurd circulation of a system where one only works to reproduce work as meaning. Everyone is still productive but only to reproduce signs!

By the mid-1970s, Baudrillard saw that this model had thrown everything into doubt. If production is a pure sign with no basis in reality, what about other codes which use production as an alibi of meaning?

Baudrillard – A Ladies' Man?

A 1977 Baudrillard critique of **Michel Foucault** (1926-84) was his launchpad for an assault on the other mirrors of production — of power, sexuality and desire.

It led to Baudrillard's exclusion from the academic influence enjoyed under the wing of the bald historian of ideas. Baudrillard was now an intellectual outlaw!

Forget Foucault!

I would have more problems remembering Baudrillard.

Foucault's Idea of Power

Foucault's mission was to ask how **discourses** and practices are implicated in the exercise of **power**. The **history of sexuality** can be described not simply in terms of who has power and who is dominated or repressed, but in terms of power as a dense transfer point for **relations** of power — from psychiatric texts to the religious confession or to gay rights.

My conclusion is that power does not censor discourses of sex. This **repressive hypothesis** of "censorship" conceals the fact that society and power **produce** discourses of sexuality.

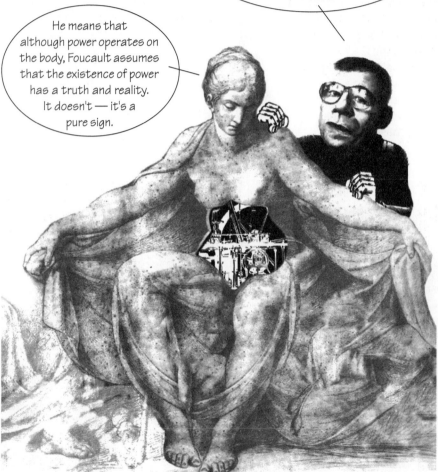

Foucault is the last great dinosaur of the classical age. He tracks down power to its most minute detail, but can't see that power, sexuality and the body are **dead**.

He means that although power operates on the body, Foucault assumes that the existence of power has a truth and reality. It doesn't — it's a pure sign.

Foucault can only see the **PRODUCTION** of sex as discourse.
Foucault assumes the body has no other reality than that of the sexual and productive model.
This circulation of the psychic, sexual and the body is a replica of the force of market value. Sexuality is an ideal means to make us manage a type of capital — sexual, unconscious, psychic and libidinal.

Male vs. Female

Baudrillard thought
this "sex capital"
rationality had
produced a radical
distinction between
male and female
which produced
the sexual
objectification of
the feminine.
All symbolic exchange
— ambivalence — had
been liquidated to the
profit of the functional
binary male/female.

Even the sexual revolution — liberation of desire and equality gives only a terroristic and abstracted sign of freedom, which circulates around the binary opposition between the sexes.

It's beside the point to debate about repression **of** sex, but rather repression **through** sex when it is employed as a **positive** sign of production or freedom.

Baudrillard introduces a comparison to symbolic cultures where sex is not an end in itself and not a production of value.

Instead, it is a long process of seduction in which sexuality is one service among others, a long procedure of gifts and countergifts. Love-making is only the eventual outcome of this reciprocity.

The traditional woman's sexuality was neither repressed nor forbidden. She was not defeated, not passive, nor did she dream of sexual liberation. To talk about sexuality in feudal, rural, and primitive societies is foolish — there has never truly been any sexuality.

It is a simulacrum.

The Disaster of Liberation

For us sex has no symbolic meaning — the sexual has become the staging of desire in a moment of pleasure. Ours is the culture of premature ejaculation.

Baudrillard asks us, what should we do after the "orgy" of sexual permissiveness — the **desublimation** of repressed desires, following the 1960s?

Answer: see it as a disaster leading to an oppression which parades as liberation. Feminism is caught in this "staging of desire".

The imperative for immediate realization of desire. Repression and liberation are part of this code.

Exaltation of the feminine is the perfect instrument of the controlled extension of sexual reason.

Against Feminism

Feminism is trapped in the sexual order dominated by **phallic values.**
The women's movement participates in the already obsolete depth models
of sexual truth and profundity. With liberation, emancipation and struggle they
accept the essentially masculine in order to supply opposing signs.

Psychoanalysis is also party to this conspiracy.

The shroud of psychoanalysis has fallen over seduction — the shroud of hidden meanings and of a hidden excess of meaning.

Women were now being taught to demand everything in order to desire
nothing, to produce the female as a sex with equal rights and pleasures and
female as value.

Feminists want to make everything speak, and they lay claims to truth and the profundity of sex — the signified of sex — sex as meaning and sex as visibility:

You've got a sexual nature and you must find out how to use it well.

You've got an unconscious and you must learn how to liberate it.

You've got a body and you must know how to enjoy it.

You've got a libido and you must know how to spend it.

Sex today is lost in its overproduction of signs. Sex is everywhere except in sexuality. There is no more prohibition.

Baudrillard condemns the feminist **Luce Irigaray** (b. 1932) for her celebration of sexual difference.

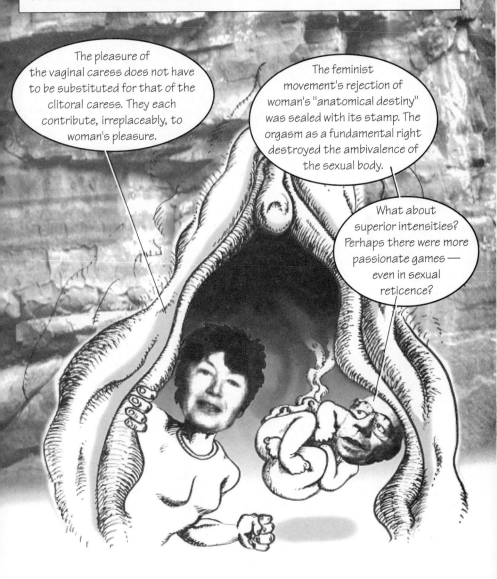

Baudrillard thought women should escape the positive and productive sign of sexual as "truth". They must be seductive!

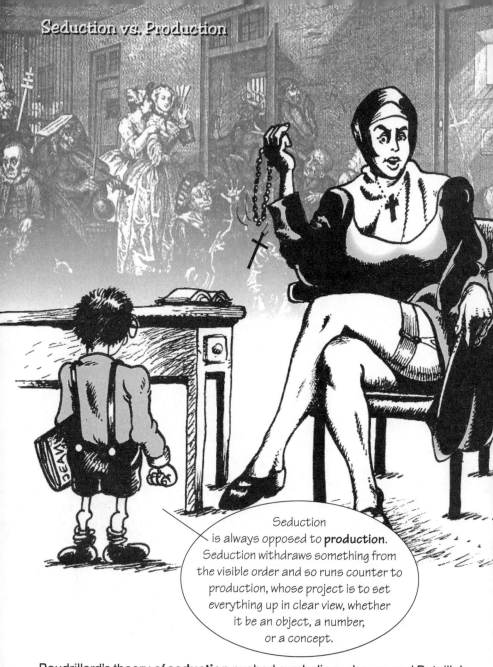

Seduction is always opposed to **production**. Seduction withdraws something from the visible order and so runs counter to production, whose project is to set everything up in clear view, whether it be an object, a number, or a concept.

Baudrillard's theory of **seduction** pushed symbolic exchange and Bataille's destruction into new territory.

Seduction is essentially a game of appearances between a subject and object (usually people, but it describes other subject-object relations). Seduction is a circular process of challenge, one-upmanship, and **death**.

94

Objects seduce by appearances. We are charmed by their seductive secrecy, mystery and artifice, and their signs challenge our claims to truth, meaning and power. But seduction does not subvert power. It is a reversible game which the object plays against the subject. It is the radical irony of objects to reverse, divert, seduce, displace, recuperate all desires of the subject.

And women do this best:

The feminine is not just seduction — it's a challenge to the male to be the sex, to monopolize sex and take it unto death.

The End of Phallocracy?

Phallocracy is collapsing under the pressure of this challenge.
Power wants to be real. Seduction doesn't. But behind power there is a void.
Inject reversibility into our economical, political, institutional or sexual
machinery and everything collapses — including male power.

Games of Seduction

So seduction is a game in continuous reciprocal exchange — and not just about sexual strategies. Seduction can end in sex, but can exhaust itself in defiance and "death" — a dizzy spiral of responses and counter-responses.

Seducer and seduced are enmeshed in a ritual of reciprocal exchange, raising the stakes in a game that never ends, because the dividing line that separates the victor and the defeated is illegible. There's no limit!

Baudrillard's tips for success...

Never say to someone, "I desire you." Say, "You make me feel very good". This turns the "object" into a subject.

Say, "Tell me who I am." Become a blank. The man then loses his power by answering.

We assume that the subject who seduces **dominates** the object who is seduced, but the object can reverse this and catch the subject in the game of appearances.

A man is trying to seduce a woman.

Next day, he receives a bloody eye in the post... By returning, upping the challenge and destroying meaning, she "fatally" seduces him.

Appearances vs. Reality

Signs of **appearance** are preferable to signs which try to take hold of reality.

Take gambling. In gambling, money is seduced, deflected from its truth and meaning. Once transformed into a stake, it's no longer a sign — it's a challenge, not an investment.

Drag queens with moustaches from Barcelona: a counter-challenge to the female model by female games. But parody doesn't mean hostility. Its play invalidates masculinity — it too enters the game. Here signs are separated from biological signifieds and become a game of appearances.

Then there are screen idols. All stars are feminine. Stars dazzle in their absence, in the coldness and non-sense of a face purged of all expression which plays out a ritualized appearance.

Stars must die, or already be dead, so that they can be perfect. In fact, death itself is pure appearance.

Feminists strike back!

101

Sentimental Cannibalism

Baudrillard's anti-humanism goes to extremes...

1981: Japanese man Issei Sagawa has dinner with a Dutch girl. He shoots her as she reads to him. Then he eats her, while professing undying love.

Baudrillard sees this "sacrifice" as the cruel seduction by the woman as object — whom the subject takes literally by effacing poetic metaphors of love and sending the game to a fateful conclusion.

Criticism:
But surely the **subject** is the cruel "seducer" here. What possible reciprocal role could the woman have? She is a murder victim!

Baudrillard and Simulation

In 1981, Jean published his infamous death-blow to reality. His claim was that reality no longer emitted signs which guarantee its existence. Signs now construct the real as **SIMULATIONS.**

Where is reality behind all the signs of production of culture, sexuality, need, use, desire?

It is no longer relevant to say the real world "exists". No system of representation or analysis can refer to the reality.

Baudrillard's **orders of simulacra** (images, semblances) chart the increasing circulation of signs, their domination and then replacement of the real. But this view must be plotted against his nostalgia for the symbolic order. A phase (feudal, medieval, primitive) when signs had an unproblematic status and reality was not in question.

Let's see how these "orders" work...

1. Symbolic Order in cultures of scarcity...

Hierarchical system (caste, rank etc.). Signs are limited and fixed by rank, duty and obligation. No fashion system here. Social mobility and wrongful use of signs (being above or below one's station) is punished.

Reality status — reality not an issue. Signs do not yet play with social "reality". Signs are dominated by **unbreakable** and **reciprocal** symbolic order.

2. First Order of Simulacra

Dominated by **Counterfeits and false images.**
From Renaissance (15th-16th centuries) up to Industrial Revolution (late 18th century).

Bourgeois order, relatively mobile society. **Fashion** is born. **Competition** over signs succeeds statutory order. Sign is freed and refers not to obligation but to produced **signifieds** (meanings like status, wealth, prestige). Most classes enter this sign exchange.

Why counterfeit? When signs are **emancipated** from **duty**, they can pretend to be anything. They dream of the symbolic order but can only feign it or falsify it. Now signs take over all aspects of social life and provide a schematic equivalent for it.

Examples of the Counterfeit

Stucco dispels the confusion of real nature and inserts a general formal scheme. Stucco coats the world and represents everything!
The false is everywhere — fake limbs (forks), fake shirt fronts, baroque architecture, theatre, political intrigue, *trompe l'oeil*, imaginary island utopias.

Reality status: signs move from **reflecting a basic reality** to **masking or perverting a basic reality**. But because they are false, a difference can be detected between semblance and reality.

This is the **natural law** of value.

3. Second Order of Simulacra

Dominated by **Production and the series**: Industrial period — 19th century.

Signs mass-produced all at once on gigantic scale by factory technology. Signs are repetitive, systematic, operational and make individuals the same (as in the system of objects). Signs now refer to serial differentiation, not to reality. To accumulate signs, one needs money, not social power.

Reality status — signs mask the absence of a basic reality and could not present it other than under the sign of **(re)production**. In the industrial series, the sign is not a counterfeit of an original, but refers instead indifferently to other signs in the series. Origin is not a concern. This is the **commercial law of value**. Marx, ideology, and use value belong here.

As does science fiction: imaginary projections of production, speed, power, energy and invention.

4. Third Order of Simulacra

Dominated by **Simulation**: current 20th century phase.

Extensive advances in science and information technology. Digitality, genetics and cybernetics are key sites of simulation. Increased use of models in all areas of culture and society.

DNA, binary code, opinion polls, referenda, marketing.

Science Fiction? No. Novels like **J.G. Ballard's** (b.1930) *Crash* (1973) — the first great novel of the universe of simulation — show that the current model of science fiction is no longer science fiction. It is **our** world — nothing is invented. In *Crash* there is neither fiction nor reality any more — hyperreality abolishes both.

Reality status — **signs bear no relation to any reality whatsoever. They are pure simulacra — simulations**.

The real returns but only in its simulation. Simulations are not appearances of reality — this would leave the **reality principle** intact.

Simulation is the collapse of the real with the imaginary, the true with the false. Simulation does not provide equivalents for the real, nor does it reproduce it — it reduplicates and generates it.

The very definition of the real becomes that of which it is possible to give an equivalent reproduction. The real is not just what can be reproduced, but what is always already reproduced. This is the **hyperreal** — the more real than real.

Here are some comparative examples of the mutation of a sign through the orders of simulacra.

1. **Counterfeit** — the **automaton**. Plays with reality — questions humanness, soul, mortality. An obvious but theatrical **fake**.

2. **Production** — the **robot**. Equivalent to man but only as abstract operational process. No interrogation of humanity or appearance. It's origin or "real" is mechanical efficiency — a triumph of dead work over real labour.

3. **Simulation** — the **clone, android** or **replicant**.
Not equivalent to man, but the generation of the real by its model (DNA, digital and electronic technologies). Collapse of difference between the true and the false, replacement by hyperreal — more human than human.

Michael Jackson — genetically baroque gender-bender or mutantly postracial?

Changing skin colour demonstrates the technological progression of simulacra. Tanning, for example, was once achieved with an artificial use of the natural sun, then produced by lamps, and later by pills, hormones and chemicals. Soon we will intervene at the genetic level to get that bronzed look!

Simulation is a panic-stricken production of the real.

When the real is no longer what it used to be, nostalgia assumes its full meaning.

Simulation resurrects myths of origin and authenticity — and "lived" experience. It threatens the real by simulating it.

Cloning is the last stage of the history and modelling of the body. Reduced to its abstract and genetic formula, the individual is destined to serial propagation.

1971: The Philippine government return a few dozen Tasaday tribespeople discovered deep in the jungle — to protect them from their "decomposition" by contact with the modern world. The Tasaday, "frozen" in their environment, were a perfect alibi to hide the fact that we are all Tasadays — living specimens under science. The irony is that the object dies in its simulation, and so kills the science that attempts to preserve signs of the real.

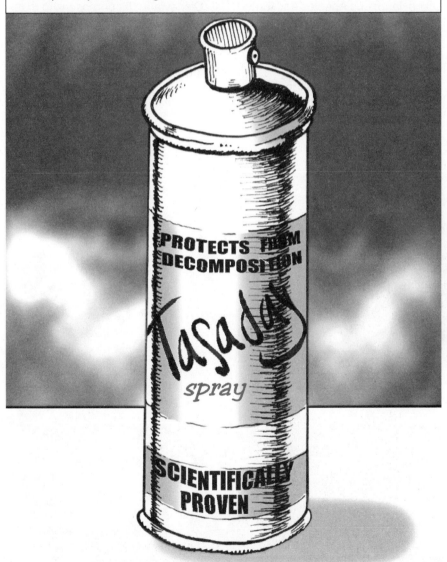

Disneyland or Baudrillard?

It's easy to read the ideology of **Disneyland** — a perfect representation of the American way of life. **But this hides a third-order simulation**.

Disneyland camouflages the fact that "real" America is itself Disneyland. Los Angeles and the America surrounding it are no longer real — just simulated. So childish behaviour is not confined to Magic Mountain. Infantile degeneration **is** the U.S.A. Disneyland and other "imaginary stations" conceal this.

Simulation is not a question of the truth or falsity of signs like Disneyland. Its purpose is to mask the fact that real is not real — to ensure that the **reality principle** is not threatened. This is the **alibi** of simulation.

Watergate

Nixon's corruption was not a scandal — only a simulation of one to conceal the fact that its condemnation by the press plays the same game of defending principles of moral and political reality.

It hides the fact that scandal no longer exists. Capitalism wants us merely to treat Watergate as immoral and to denounce it in morality's name — ensuring capital's survival.

Simulation destroys cause and effect, origins, continuity and dialectics.

I am not a crook!

Holograms claim to be closer to the real — but why should they? In fact, they make us sensitive to the fact that everything escapes representation, its own double and its resemblance. So there is no real.

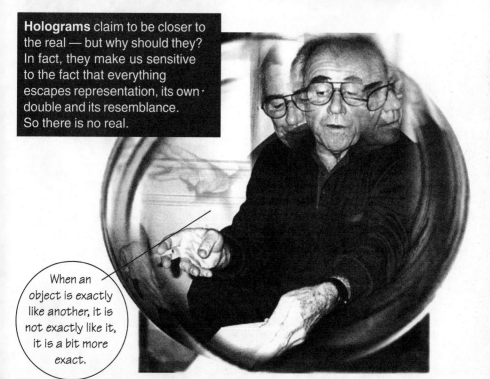

When an object is exactly like another, it is not exactly like it, it is a bit more exact.

The Bomb that Destroyed Reality

1980: A bombing in Italy...
Who caused it and why?
Leftist extremists, or ultra right-
wing provocation, or centrists
who want to bring terrorist
extremes into disrepute, or
perhaps the police did it to get a
bigger budget?

In simulation this is all true.
And even if we find out the real
"truth" — this vertigo of
interpretation is not stemmed...

In simulation, all signs are interchangeable. This is because simulation is
generated by a **precession of the model**. The model comes first — the
prior existence of codes like power and media. The "fact" — the bombing
— arises from these models. This is the **Moebius strip** of twisting
meaning where front is back and true is false.

And, of course, because the real is no longer possible — illusion is impossible. The poles of true and false collapse into one another.

It would be difficult and dangerous to fake a hold-up, not only because your phoney fire-arm and artificial demands will be met with the violence of the law, but because you are suggesting that law and order might be nothing more than simulation! The law replies by treating your robbery as real, and shooting you.

It was only a joke! It's not a real gun! I'm not an alien!

The real devours any attempt at simulation. It can't deal with it as simulation, just as the army prefers to take a person simulating madness for a real madman. Because the real cannot isolate or identify simulation, we can no longer isolate or define the real itself!

Because the economy is simulated, there will never be financial collapse. Simulation acts as **deterrence.**

In **1987**, the stock market collapsed, but nothing real happened. Capitalism today is in "orbit" as simulation, and leaves the world intact. If it came back down to earth, economic exchange would freeze.
Its circulation stops money becoming real again and so prevents catastrophe. This is **virtual capitalism**!

Deterrence is what causes something not to take place.

A Simulated Education.

Universities were formerly sites of challenge to power. Knowledge — or its destruction by radical students — had meaning. Today, universities are simulacra — worthless diplomas circulate like Eurodollars without any real equivalence in work or knowledge. All squabbles between tutors and students are nostalgic yearnings for a time when knowledge was a real stake.

No Nukes

The ultimate in simulation is nuclear weaponry. The menace of destruction is not the real issue — it is the **precession** of the real war by a system of signs of destruction which makes their use meaningless. Nuclear war will not take place. Deterrence is circulated among protesters and governments like money or signs putting an end to real war.

The simulation model of nuclear deterrence turns real life into ephemeral scenarios of survival and pointless violence. Entirely neutralized, the whole planet is made useless by this "hypermodel" of international security.

Nuclear weapons — the best system of control that never existed!

What about nuclear accidents such as Chernobyl and Harrisburg?

Baudrillard says that simulations of nuclear catastrophe and films like the ***China Syndrome*** precede and contaminate incidents like Harrisburg. In fact, the film is the real event and Harrisburg is the simulacrum. Catastrophe is deterred and distilled. The only chain reaction taking place is the implosive spectacle of the media.

IT COULD BE YOU!

Baudrillard published three articles on the **Gulf War** in *Libération* (4.1.91 — 29.3.91). Before its outbreak, he claimed it would not take place. Afterwards, on TV, he claimed he was right — the Gulf War had not happened! His point is not that nothing took place, but that what took place wasn't a war. It was non-war — a deterrence to war. Here's why...

There was no enemy — Saddam Hussein was an accomplice to the USA's intervention in the Middle East. His soft terrorism helped the west dispel the hard terrorism of Palestinians, etc. He was already beholden to outside forces.

There were no warriors involved, only hostages: Saddam's "guests" and CNN's audience — **us**.

There was rarely direct conflict, and its outcome was predictable. The methods and technologies of each side were not opposed but radically different, resulting in a pre-programmed act of policing in response to a Third World dictator who fought like it was still World War II!

This means war!

As simulation, the invasion of Kuwait and its "liberation" could be represented in any way — as the ambition of a local dictator, or the plot by America to legitimize its intervention in the region.

It was a virtual war of information, electronics and images — not primarily of force. The more we had access to "live" war events, the more the reality became information — which quickly affected how the event was conducted. Most of the journalists at the "front" got their information from CNN.

The "enemy" was not challenged or annihilated. Saddam was left in place to ensure USA interests were intact. He was allowed to crush Kurds and Shiites.

Baudrillard was offered a job of covering the Gulf War, but refused, saying, "I live in the virtual. Send me into the real and I don't know what to do. And anyway what would I have seen? Those who went there saw nothing, only odds and ends... Non-war is the absence of politics continued by other means."

And no principle was saved, other than deterrence. The subsequent "peace" is also a simulation.

Criticism:
Christopher Norris: Absurd — a postmodern mood of widespread cynical acquiescence.

Criticism:
Disgraceful — people died! Where's Baudrillard's humanity?

What is happening on the ground there in Iraq, it's so vile. It's enough to drive you either into depression or into a rage. As an abstract problem of simulation the war is exciting, but in the real I experience the same anger as others.

Simulation was driving me nuts.

His book **The Gulf War Did Not Take Place** — and perhaps the conflict itself — was the culmination of ten years' work on simulation.

Baudrillard and the Media

Cutting through all Baudrillard's work is his uneasy relationship to the mass media and communications — the frontlines of the sign. The "real" Baudrillard doesn't quite know what to think...

But his answerphone in his central Paris apartment is always on, and he appears on TV to present his ideas to the masses.

I'm truly incapable of recording anything in a *tête-à-tête* with a machine.

Baudrillard - the French McLuhan?

Herbert Marshall McLuhan (1911- 80), the Canadian culturologist, has had a great influence on Baudrillard. His investigations of the psychological and social effects of media point to a simple conclusion — THE MEDIUM IS THE MESSAGE.

The personal and social consequences of any medium result from the new scale that is introduced into our affairs by each extension of ourselves, or by any new technology.

Baudrillard started to demolish socialist theories of media while avoiding McLuhan's delirious "tribal optimism" — his "global village".

Many neo-Marxist theories, such as **Hans Magnus Enzenberger's**, see productive forces and technology as holding the promise of human fulfilment which capitalism has confiscated.

No! The media do not communicate a prior dominant ideology as false messages to the masses. The ideology is in the form of the media itself in the social division it establishes. The mass media fabricate non-communication.

Baudrillard reverts to symbolic exchange. Real communication exists when there is a reciprocal space for speech and response, and a personal responsibility or duty.

In the mass media this cannot exist, despite all the "transmission-reception" models communication theorists use. No response is possible.

Take the linguist **Roman Jakobson's** (1896-1982) theoretical model.

Baudrillard argues that the first and last terms are separated and reunited artificially. There is no reciprocal relation. Only one person communicates while the other receives the message. There's no ambivalence, just a simulation model of communication.

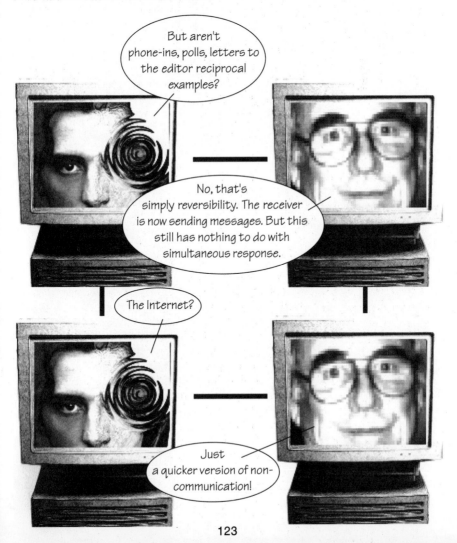

The Medium is the Model

So, is there any liberating potential in the media?

No. Take May '68 in France.

The mass media chain-reacted and sent out the revolutionary messages. But the form of the media made the contents abstract and universal.

The strike was exported to all corners of France as a model of action with one single meaning. Not the lived, spontaneous strike of real life.

Now the **medium is not the message** — it's the **model**. Transformed into media models (like the news), the symbols of resistance were short-circuited. Subversive acts such as strikes are no longer produced except as a function of their reproducibility.

Reciprocity — real communication rather than codes — will only happen with the destruction of the media.

People meet their neighbours for the first time while watching their apartments burn down.

What about the contents of the media?

Let's take advertising. Advertising doesn't fool us or lie. It's beyond this, because its arguments are neither true nor false. It would be impossible to gauge their accuracy, since their origins do not lie in reality. Advertising is its own truth — a self-fulfilling prophecy. This is all reality is these days!

Advertising - A Dead Language

Advertising has no depth — it is the "degree zero" of meaning. Today we have **absolute advertising**, imposed everywhere from politics to economics. But its dilution means its disappearance. The power of advertising language has been stolen by the processing language of computer science. Digitality is more thrilling.

The more real images seem, the more **diabolical** they become. This is the **Evil Demon of Images** —

Of all the spectacles, it's the only one I like.

Baudrillard is a movie fan, although he hates art cinema and its "voyeuristic coteries". The first film he ever walked out from was documentary filmmaker **François Reichenbach's** (b.1922) *Houston, Texas — Le Grand Sud* (1956).

It all went on a bit too long and I left.

In film Baudrillard sees many examples of the implosion of image and "reality" played out. For instance, **Francis Ford Coppola's** (b.1939) *Apocalypse Now* (1979). The film was made in the same way Americans fought the Vietnam War — the same technological feats, monstrous honesty and psychedelic fantasy. It makes the Vietnam War seem a rehearsal or test site for the many movies that came in its wake.

During filming, the borrowed helicopters had to break off to reinforce real troops in the Philippine forests. Add the life-threatening schedule, the virtual psychoses of the actors and the millions spent and you have all the signs of war!

Who won the Vietnam War?

Both sides. Vietnam got the ideological and political victory and America sent *Apocalypse Now* around the world.

Baudrillard prefers cinema to TV. He only recently invested in a set. Here's why... "My point of view is that of the screen..."

TV is endless play. Constant channel-surfing is pure fascination. One is never seduced and there's no fun in it — just function.

Compare a real football match to a televized one. The first is "hot", emotional and "choreographed". The second is modulated — a montage of play-backs and close-ups.

Television's cold light is no longer an image — unlike the imaginary of film with its myth and fantasy.

What's on TV tonight?

It's us dear...

"Reality TV" exhumes the real in its fundamental banality. Like the American 1971 documentary on the Loud family — seven months of uninterrupted shooting, 300 hours of non-stop broadcasting. This hyperreal family fell apart, begging the question: what would have happened if the TV cameras hadn't been there? Did they cause this reality?

Reality TV calls causality into question!

In "tele-space" there are no fixed positions. Unlike discourse, the digital world has no poles — only processing of data. Each person is his or her own terminal. TV is not communication, only connection — electronic narcosis. TV converses with itself — and we are integrated as a man-machine circuit.

The TV movie *Holocaust* — Hitler's Final Solution on the box.

It conducts neither good nor bad intentions. Extermination is replayed, but is itself cold. TV **itself** is the final solution, exterminating all meaning, origin, symbolism. The Jews this time are victims of the videotape and sound track. But the event is exorcised cheaply, for a few tears.

Reality Served Cold

To "reheat" a historical event (the Holocaust, the Cold War, V.E. Day) is to beam a cold event via a cold medium to a cold mass. The horror is made inoffensive in the posthumous shudder of TV — a "pathological reactualization of a past". TV immunizes the real.

Baudrillard is harsh on "instant history" TV.

His essay in *Libération* (7.1.94) attacks the hype of a television link-up with Sarajevo...

No pity for Sarajevo.

SARAJEVO

Computers come in for similar criticism. Virtual man is a "spastic". Intelligence conferred on computers indicates real thought has disappeared. The screen is both close and distant — too true and too false. But these machines have no artifice, no irony — except perhaps for electronic viruses by which computers might be said to parody their artificial intelligence.

The Silent Majority – Baudrillard and the Masses

1978 saw Baudrillard's inevitable abandonment of firm leftism and an apparent "bleak fatalism" in relation to his view of society — and sociology.

What's at stake here is the function of the social as a meaningful term, bound up with its signs of freedom, repression and revolution.

His earlier Marxist critique had assessed the relationship between consumer objects as signs and strategies of **class logic** — the potential discriminatory organization of consumer objects by a social group.

His work shadowed that of rival sociologist **Pierre Bourdieu** (b. 1930). Both tended to reduce consumption to class antagonism. Class was **difference**.

TV and Class

The television object demonstrated Baudrillard's interest in class as a meaningful agent in social meaning.

It is used by upper classes rarely and kept hidden. Used by middle classes for its educational value (documentaries, news). The TV is usually integrated but not central.

Used by lower classes for the pleasure its images bring. Their infinite patience in watching is usually confused with bovine passivity. They disguise their cultural inferiority by criticizing the boring (superior) nature of some programmes. The TV is covered with knick-knacks and the whole room is organized around it.

Other activities — polishing, cleaning, varnishing and other signs of over-abundance or sparsity — depict class strategies of discrimination and differentiation, usually embodying the "rhetoric of despair": a lower class's desperate attempt to aspire to signs of dominant classes.

But by 1978 Baudrillard rejected this two-step reading as a ruse. Classes do not decode a dominant group's messages or meanings of objects or images according to their own class logic, like primitive natives recycling western money in their own symbolic circulation.

This is offensive and only salvages the material disseminated by the dominant culture.

Baudrillard — then Professor of Sociology at Nanterre — turned his attack on sociology from the perspective of its object of study — **the social**.

Anti-Sociology

Sociology had survived on a definitive and positive hypothesis of the social — but its concepts were mysterious. Class, social relations, power, status, institutions and the social itself were muddled but used to preserve the code of sociology.

Baudrillard replaced the word social with the term "mass".
What's the difference?
That's the wrong question, because it would mean defining the mass or masses.

The mass is without attribute, predicate, quality or reference.

It has no sociological "reality".

Yet Baudrillard does seek to represent something:
La masse —
-can refer directly to substance or matter
-can mean the majority — as in the mass of workers
-can connote aspects of physics — the electrical usage of an "earth"
-can allude to astrophysics — the mass as a black hole or "opaque nebula".

What has happened to society?

Since the 18th century, the social was evoked as meaning by the representation made of it by politics. Before then, politics was Machiavellian — a cunning game which did not pretend to represent social truth.

Although the system continues, it no longer represents anything or has an equivalent in reality. The classical Marxist or bourgeois order of representation (a people, a class, a proletariat, relations of production) no longer operates.

The Neutral Mass

In fact, the masses resist representation by anyone. They absorb all radiation from the outlying **constellations** of State, History, Culture, Meaning. They are inertia — the **strength of the neutral**.

Attempts by the media to get meaning across to the masses — to inform, socialize or educate — are resisted.

Criticism: But that means the masses are mystified...?

Baudrillard: "No, you then assume that they would aspire to the natural light of reason, if they only knew it. It is in complete freedom that the masses **refuse** meaning."

Take a French scenario. Activist Klaus Croissant is extradited. On the night, 20,000,000 people are glued to their TVs watching France win a World Cup qualifier. The press thought this was disgraceful. The masses shouldn't be indifferent to a political crisis!

Baudrillard: What contempt in this reading. Why are there so many "pacified" people who, without even asking themselves why, frankly prefer a football match to a human and political drama?

The Silent Majority

So what's left?

The silent majority — a statistical beacon placed at the horizon of a "disappeared social". Their representation is no longer possible. They do not express a reality — they are now surveyed, tested, polled. The social is now a model. Dialogue or dialectic between "class" and its representation by "politics" is over — now there is only confusion of these poles.

Then who's winning? The simulation of power which employs the masses to mean something? Or the simulation of the social which the masses use against power?

No-one knows — and the masses don't care...

Statistics "produces" the mass as an anticipated response. We all know how statistics can be manipulated and conclusions interchanged, but what about the hyperconformity to statistics that the mass **simulates** — the same signals and the same responses?

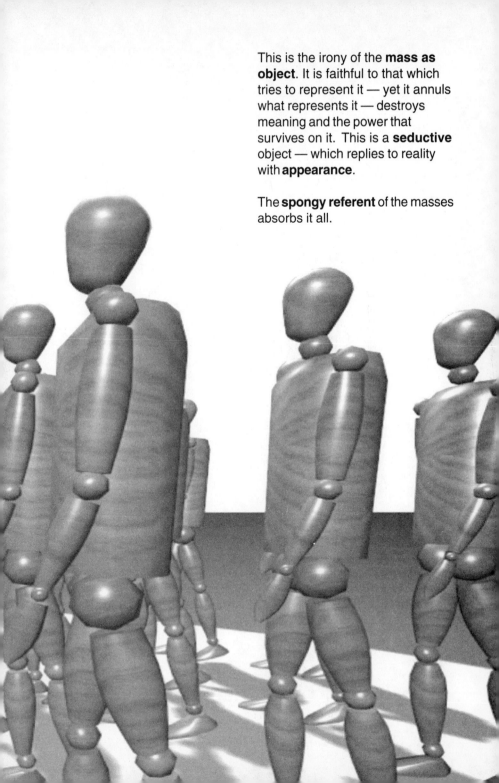

This is the irony of the **mass as object**. It is faithful to that which tries to represent it — yet it annuls what represents it — destroys meaning and the power that survives on it. This is a **seductive** object — which replies to reality with **appearance**.

The **spongy referent** of the masses absorbs it all.

Implosion

The trouble is that it's gone too far and reached **fatal** speed. Implosion spells the end of every representation and its violent intake as non-meaning.

Implosion implies **anti-representative, anti-universalist** tendencies. Including communes, drugs and weird religious cults (David Koresh).

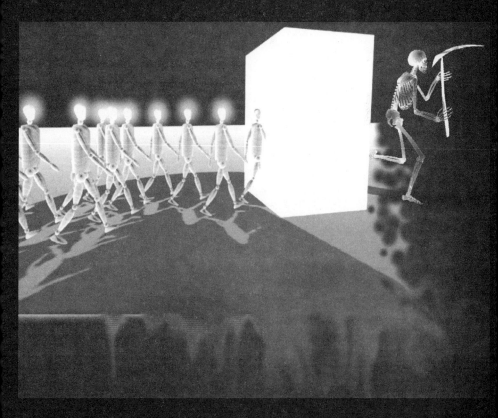

A definition of the social? A residue — an **excremental accumulation of death** — ready to be recycled. But as usual, social surplus wreaks an ironic revenge.

The messages of the media are devoured by the masses. This may spell the disappearance of the media as a meaningful term. No more medium, no more message. Sorry McLuhan...

A World of Residues?

The **Remainder** is Baudrillard's term for what is excluded or "residue", such as the nonsocialized groups in society like the crazy, or waste in art, pollution, or repression. But today this accumulation of weak, marginal remainders is being sponged up and used by the social system.

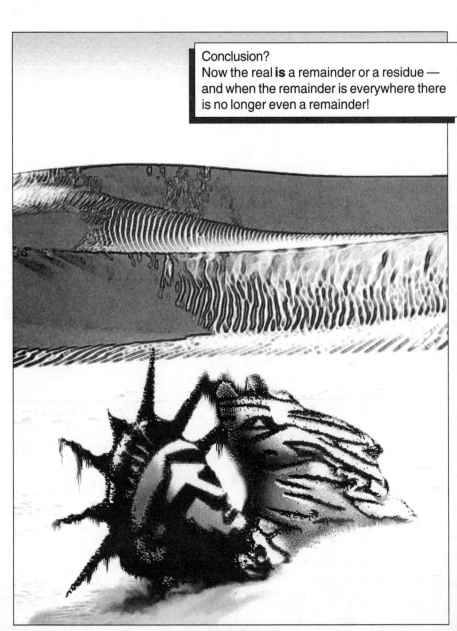

Conclusion?
Now the real **is** a remainder or a residue — and when the remainder is everywhere there is no longer even a remainder!

So where is politics today?

Revolution, class misfortune and the curse of capitalism have been superseded by love, care, togetherness, compassion, selflessness.

The new "look" generation — successful in everything, religiously and casually supports human rights, dissidence, anti-racism, anti-nuclear movement and the environment. Their insipid "remakes" include liberal Marxism — the "divine" left of socialism, green politics and soft feminism. European yuppies can support Live Aid, shed tears, and still turn up for work on Monday morning.

But Baudrillard is ironic: "I don't believe in the ecological movement, but I do it."

And he provides strong analyses of the present European New Order. Why has ultra-right Le Pen disappeared from the political scene? Because his racist ideas have infiltrated the political system. It's no good looking at Bosnia and warning that ethnic cleansing could happen elsewhere. White "integrism", protectionism, discrimination and control are already with us...

Baudrillard's Fatal Decision

Baudrillard's destruction of the social left a question.

How could theory represent the world when representation was impossible?
The masses had taught him that they could outstrip any representation made of them. And social theory would be implicated.

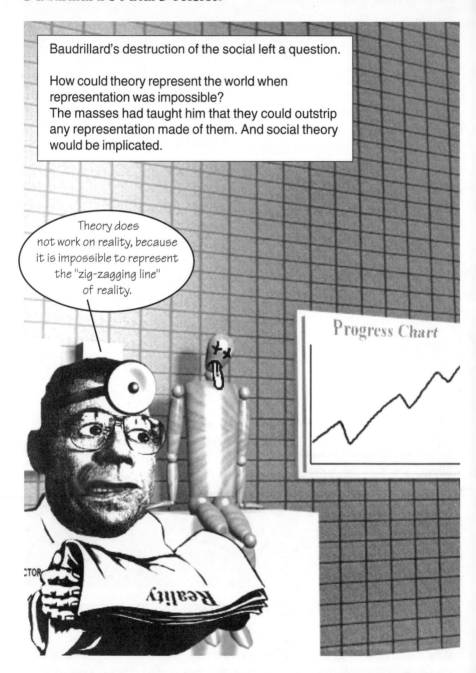

Theory does not work on reality, because it is impossible to represent the "zig-zagging line" of reality.

Progress Chart

Theory in the age of the object must forget about **representing** the world. It must assume the form of a world where truth has **receded**.

144

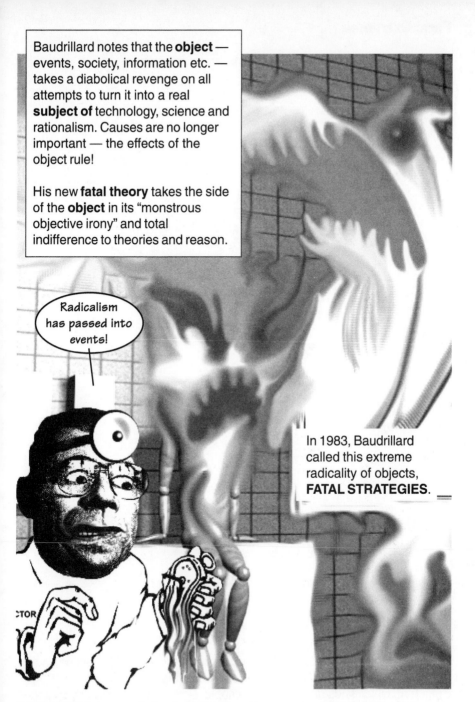

Baudrillard notes that the **object** — events, society, information etc. — takes a diabolical revenge on all attempts to turn it into a real **subject of** technology, science and rationalism. Causes are no longer important — the effects of the object rule!

His new **fatal theory** takes the side of the **object** in its "monstrous objective irony" and total indifference to theories and reason.

Radicalism has passed into events!

In 1983, Baudrillard called this extreme radicality of objects, **FATAL STRATEGIES**.

Fatal strategies are not simply resistances to power or meaning. Their strategies are to exacerbate, redouble, escalate, ironize and thus escape the will of the subject. This is the **evil genius** of the **object**.

Fatal Extremes

Here's how fatal strategies move to extremes.

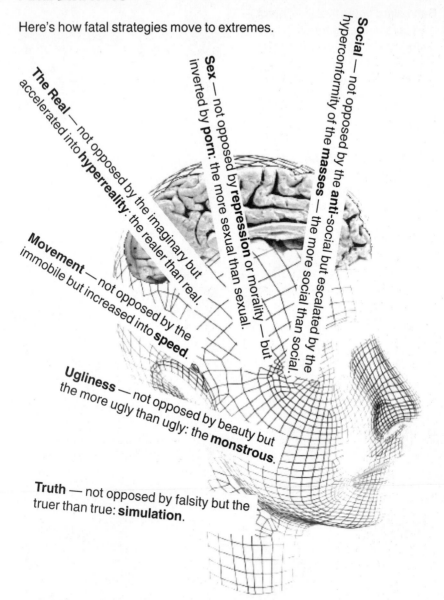

Social — not opposed by the **anti**-social but escalated into hyperconformity of the **masses** — the more social than social.

Sex — not opposed by **repression** or morality — but inverted by **porn**: the more sexual than sexual.

The Real — not opposed by the imaginary but accelerated into **hyperreality**: the realer than real.

Movement — not opposed by the immobile but increased into **speed**.

Ugliness — not opposed by beauty but the more ugly than ugly: the **monstrous**.

Truth — not opposed by falsity but the truer than true: **simulation**.

Don't forget "extreme revulsions":
"Allergies" such as terrorism, drugs and delinquency speak of rejection and negation — a kind of exorcism and a form of disgust.
But a form which finds nothing unacceptable. Nowadays you seduce a woman with the words, "I am interested in your c**t."
The same with art, which is reduced to the remark: "What we want from you is stupidity and bad taste."

Holidaymakers seek a fatal strategy. As subjects resisting the boredom of everyday life, you would expect them obediently to follow "voluntary servitude" with the **banal strategy** of happiness and distraction. But no — on vacation in their hyper-banality they **redouble** their boredom. They want something excessive — and **boredom** ironizes everyday life.

The object always avoids what's good for it!

Adapt sidewalks to allow access to motorized disabled people. The blind who used the curb as a guide get run over. So handrails are installed for the blind. Then handicapped people get their wheelchairs caught on these rails.

Ecstasy

Baudrillard's vocabulary of the 1980s describes the way in which the subject's modern alienation has been succeeded by the object's **ecstasy of communication.**

Objects in the universe of **information** are ecstatic. Ecstasy is the quality of any body that spins until all its sense disappears, until it shines out as a pure and empty form in a **vertiginous** universe.

Fashion: an ecstatic version of beauty which spells beauty's disappearance. If clothes were truly beautiful, there would be no fashion. Fashion's beauty absorbs its opposite — ugliness — in the ecstatic exchange of one season's wardrobe for the next.

More Ecstasy . . .

The American government asks the multinational Exxon for a general report on its activities worldwide. The company delivers twelve volumes of a thousand pages each, which would take years to read and longer to analyze.

In the ecstatic world, meaning is not lacking. There is **too much** of it. Information engorges the world.

The Obscene

The obscene begins when illusion or spectacle disappears and everything becomes exposed to the raw, inescapable light of information. The obscene is the **more visible than visible.** But the obscene is not confined to sex or porn, and not always "hot", organic, carnal or visceral. The **cool obscenity** of the world is superficial, **fascinating** and saturated with information. When everything is on show, there are no more secrets or ambiguities — just information exposed by science, media and technology in **rituals of transparency**.

Baudrillard gives us an eye-full in his example of the Japanese **vaginal cyclorama**. This is not a seductive strip-tease. Prostitutes sit with legs open on the edge of a platform. Japanese workers are permitted to shove their faces into the lined-up vaginas to see better. But to see what?

Like Duane Hanson's **hyperrealist** sculpture. People peer at the skin of these figures, the total visibility of realness, and want to "test" them.

Obscene images and objects have nothing to see in them — except the useless objectivity of things. There's no game or challenge here, so it's **not** seduction.

What sort of person inhabits this universe? We do — as **schizophrenics**. Not in the clinical sense of losing touch with reality, but with the screen. The confusion of someone who is open to the over-proximity of all things.

Trans-Everything

We no longer know who we are. Graffiti artists know this. Once they wrote:

"I exist, my name is So-and-So, I live in New York." Signs pregnant with meaning.

Today "tagging" is indecipherable: "I exist but I have no name and nothing to say."

The **transpolitical** enters the fray. This describes the breaking up and mixing of all categories of culture which now flaunt themselves in a universe which is without structure.

The **transexual** breaks down the boundary between male and female.
The **transaesthetic**: the boundary between art and anti-art.

When everything that meant something has gone — politics, body, sex — the transpolitical remains, just to show all this has disappeared.

Bio-Terminology: Hypertelia

The transpolitical defines the route from growth to tumorous replication. Baudrillard uses terminology which alludes to biology and neurology.
Hypertelia — a process of something surpassing its function or objective, like cancer cells reproducing too quickly. Our daily lives are cancerous — all effects of communication, information, production and destruction have turned from their allotted course and destination.

Maybe not...
Perhaps this ecstatic proliferation keeps something safe — the reality principle.

AIDS does this. It's the loss of antibodies, but is also an antibody to society. It thwarts the catastrophic logic of global systems by providing an accelerated catastrophe — thus keeping the "body social" meaningful.

AIDS, computer viruses and terrorism are examples of superconductive events — excessive phenomena which affect not just countries, individuals or institutions but entire structures: sex, money, information, communications... AIDS is certainly a sort of crash in sexual values, while computers played a "virulent" role in the Wall Street Crash of 1987.

Metastasis

Metastasis: when a body is deprived of meaning, soul and metaphor and is an organization of excitable circuits, neurons and chromosomes — programmes in excitable suspense waiting to switch on — waiting for the ecstatic moment of mutation.

This anticipation is present in physical handicaps. Disabled people are like the advance guard who experiment with the body, brain and senses in preparation for the inhuman and abnormal universe we are all plunging into.

Blind people play a ball game called "torball" in which they exhibit posthuman sci-fi telepathic reflexes.

Anomaly

Anomaly — a loss of faith in the norm and its proliferation in mutation...

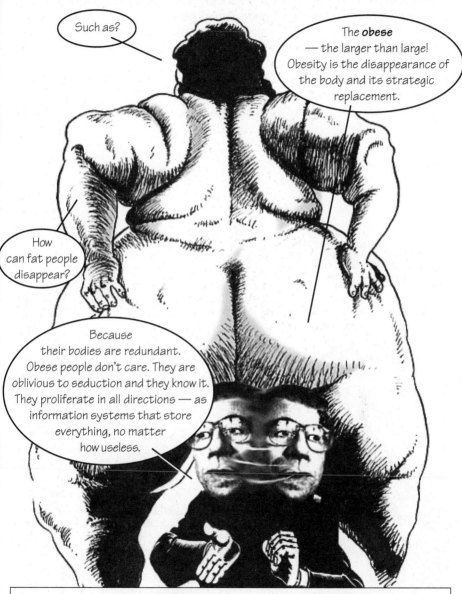

The obese put an end to sex by absorbing it. They want only to divide into two, to make sex look redundant.

Like **clones**, they're produced as sexual beings, but of course their sex is superfluous. Sex becomes a dead difference — pure excess.

Terrorism is an ecstatic form of violence — as spectacle. It doesn't oppose State violence with meaning (it makes ridiculous demands and never wins at this level). Terrorism can only work if it exterminates meaning — which sustains the State — by producing senseless acts which **accelerate** the senselessness of power.
The struggle should be fought against meaning by providing a **virulent excess** of reality.

No meaning is necessary. In fact there is no need for terrorists to do anything. There are terrorists who do no more than claim responsibility for aeroplane accidents from the comfort of their armchairs. The media does the rest...

So today the world is sworn to extremes. It does not oppose meanings, it hypes them. This radical antagonism does not reconcile the object and the subject. Baudrillard calls this the **principle of Evil** — the object in its ecstatic form destroys the subject.

Like? The ultimate "evil" negation of all western values: the Ayatollah's symbolic utterance of the fate of Salman Rushdie.

Scary! Baudrillard is building a theory which is ironic. It represents nothing, but hypersimulates the world's extreme strategies.

By 1990 Baudrillard had refined these ideas, and published them as a collection: *The Transparency of Evil — Essays in Extreme Phenomena*. Which extremes? Ex porn star and Italian MP La Cicciolina — the ideal woman of a telephone chat-line.

Baudrillard and Nietzsche's Superman?

Fatal strategies consist in sending the old world towards its destruction.

"To push that which wants to fall", said the maverick philosopher **Friedrich Nietzsche** (1844-1900). He shares with Baudrillard a style of extremes which destroys the immoral basis of morality, dispenses with metaphysical explanations, and shows the irrational tendency of rationalism.

This "aristocratic radicalism" charts a darker, more nihilistic path of modernity, where the will of the Nietzschean "superman" would force the world to realize itself in an apocalyptic moment to a "revaluation of all values".

God is dead.

Simulacra suggest a destructive truth. There has never been any God. God is not dead, he has become hyperreal.

I am a nihilist.

But not the dark, Nietzschean variety, nor the destructive, dandified Romantic kind, nor the Surrealist, Dadaist, terroristic or political nihilism of the 20th century. **Jean's nihilism is not about the destruction of meaning, but of its disappearance**.

But the spirit of Nietzsche hovers over Baudrillard's recent work, particularly his style and aphorisms.

Baudrillard began to write in fragments. Disconnected writing is indifferent to its truth and purpose — and it is disruptive of claims of finding a central point.

Examples...

Baudrillard's style alters radically from the late 1970s as he produces a poetic writing to give form to the disappearance of real.

Baudrillard on Tour...

He started to keep a diary from about 1980 and travelled extensively, lecturing, driving and taking snaps. Now he had new objects to write about — **entire countries**!

America, Australia, Argentina, Brazil, Thailand...

Demands for interviews reached panic levels when he published his "diary" *Cool Memories* (1987) and travelogue *Amerique* (1986).

Cool Memories encapsulated his musings on the women in his life, his indifference to a Stevie Wonder concert, the western contamination of Aboriginals by the deadly virus of origins and the stupidity of OAPs on a jetplane.

The books brought him a new audience. *The Guardian* (21.9.88) asked, "Who is Jean Baudrillard?"

Journalist Brian Rotman: "A prophet of the apocalypse? Hysterical lyricist of panic?"

And samples of his aphorisms appeared in the first edition of *The European* (11.5.90).

ROUTE
66

USA

With travel, appearances and writing Baudrillard retired from teaching sociology at the University of Nanterre in 1987.

Nihilist for hire...

His travelogue is like a travelling shot from his automobile where speed cancels out the ground beneath him.

I wasn't looking for the depth of social and cultural America — but for the America of pure circulation — freeways, desert speed, screenplays and television: ASTRAL AMERICA.

"The Desert of the Real"

A tourist with no sights to visit and no destination... What's his strategy? To gauge the superficiality of America against the depth of Europe. To treat the States as the "last primitive society of the future" — beyond history. To use the desert as a metaphor for the disappearance of the social and culture. It preserves insignificance and indifference, is magical and banal. Desert includes the cities as well as salt flats.

So what is Baudrillard's America like?

America for Baudrillard is utopia — a world present and complete. America is a woman, unfamiliar and disappearing. America is cinematic. America is the end of the world and the catastrophe — the extermination and disappearance of meaning.

The inhumanity of our ulterior, asocial, superficial world immediately finds its aesthetic form here, in its ecstatic form.

Let's take some snapshots of
Baudrillard's "desert of the real".

Salt Lake City — where all the
Christs look like Bjorn Borg.
New York — where people
smile — but only to
themselves.
Grand Canyon —
a geologically
metaphysical slow-
motion
catastrophe.
Santa Cruz —
paradise — but a
very slight
modification
would suffice to make
it seem like hell.
Los Angeles — as soon
as you start walking, you
are a threat to public order.

Breakdancers — digging a hole for themselves within their own bodies — the pose of the dead.
Jogging — a new form of voluntary servitude and a new form of adultery.
Death Valley — a place of sacrifice, secrecy. If something has to disappear here, to match the desert for its beauty, why not a woman?

Critics enjoyed his book. For instance, Doug Kellner: "Ludicrous, banal, racist, cliché, condescending, and aggressively sexist — a projection of Baudrillard's own fantasies." **America** may be "symptomatic of the decline of Baudrillard's theoretical powers and the collapse of social analysis and critique
— as well as politics."

Kellner: "And you probably wrote it after a few scotches."

Another critic: "A reactionary approach to race, a kind of environmental determinism — naive neo-primitivism."

Baudrillard Accused!

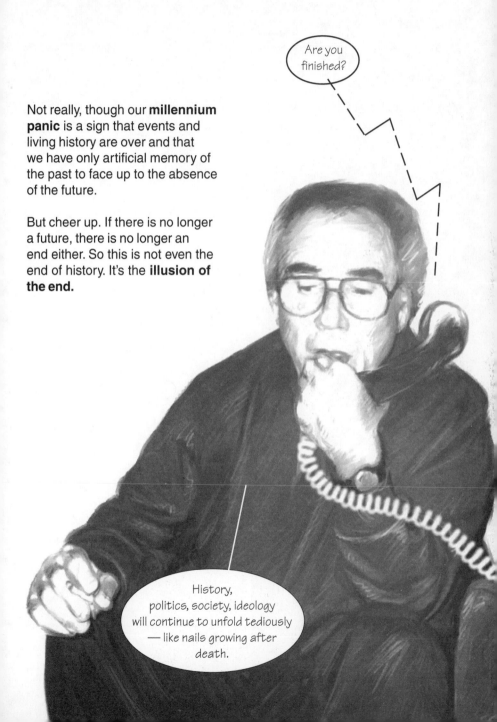

Are you finished?

Not really, though our **millennium panic** is a sign that events and living history are over and that we have only artificial memory of the past to face up to the absence of the future.

But cheer up. If there is no longer a future, there is no longer an end either. So this is not even the end of history. It's the **illusion of the end.**

History, politics, society, ideology will continue to unfold tediously — like nails growing after death.

The world is now a double spiral where concepts outlined by Baudrillard criss cross and melt into one another — production and seduction, economics and death, the fatal and the banal.

We are now in **escape velocity** and have left reality — which includes the apocalypse — behind us. Instead we are offered history and events in the technical perfection of the news. And news events are always forgotten...

Societies no longer expect anything from the future, have no confidence in history, and dig in behind technology, information stores and communications networks where time is obliterated by pure circulation of **everything**.

What are we left with?

1. Repentance as a **postmodern** recycling of past forms, like...

Contemporary art which plunders previous styles.

The same wars breaking out between the same peoples.

The reunification of Germany — showing a topsy-turvy rewriting of the 20th century.

> At the rate we are going we shall soon be back at the Holy Roman Empire.

GERMANY GERMA

This is the **deconstruction** of history.

Anyone for Recycled Fascism? It is not nostalgia for fascism that is dangerous: what is dangerous is that pathological re-enactment of the past in which everyone plays a part, in which everyone collaborates — those who deny the existence of the gas chambers just as much as those who believe in their reality.

2. The celebration of all residue...

"Freedom" is defrosted and resurrected in the Eastern Bloc after the Cold War. But freedom after the end of history will be intent on one thing — trading itself off in a binge of electrical goods, drugs and pornography. History as ultra-fluidity and circulation!

3. And eclectic sentimentality...

"Charity cannibalism"
— the caring exploitation
of poverty recycled as
new energy sources.
We enjoy the moving spectacle
of our efforts to help others. Other
people's misery is our adventure
playground. This is the last phase of
colonialism, the **New Sentimental Order.**

Our **sentimentality** towards **animals** is a sure sign of the disdain in which we hold them. The trajectory animals have followed, from divine sacrifice to dog cemeteries with atmospheric music, from sacred defiance to ecological sentimentality, speaks loudly enough of the vulgarization of the status of man himself.

From experimentation, through breeding and African reserves, animals have preceded us on the path of liberal extermination.

Postmodern Guru?

Baudrillard has been called the "high priest of postmodernism". Is he?

Postmodern theory puts modernity and modernism into question; charts the disappearance of the subject, authenticity and depth; foregrounds the problem of representation; sees reality as an effect of language; notes the disappearance of "grand narratives" such as Marxism, and describes the fragmentation or pluralism of the social.
But Baudrillard rejected the pomo label at a lecture in New York in 1986.

Postmodernism is a regression. It's the most degenerate, artificial and eclectic phase. It doesn't have a meaning. It's impossible to define what is going on now. There's a void, which I analyse.

"He is treading the well-worn paths of one type of modernist scepticism and excess. His message of 'no future' does not transcend the political dilemma of modernism, it exemplifies it." Chris Rojek

But is Baudrillard really saying, "No future"? Not quite.

"The End" as Parody

Baudrillard: "There is no end in the sense that God is dead, or history is dead. I would prefer not to play the role of the lugubrious, thoroughly useless prophet."

Baudrillard is not speaking of the real extermination of living beings. His books are scenarios in which he plays out the end of things as a complete parody.

Catastrophe is ironic. The space-shuttle disaster was a parody over catastrophe — a luxurious burial in the sky which revived our appetite for space exploration. We now have a horizontal era of events without consequences. The end of the world is rehearsed, so will never arrive.

Forget Baudrillard?

So this is Baudrillard's world — simulated, obscene, seductive, ecstatic, a world without hope because hope implies a future, which is now only a newscast. But the question remains: Is this a world we can accept? If not, what should we do about it?

Bibliography

Jean Baudrillard — Selected Texts

(1975)   *The Mirror of Production,*
          St Louis: Telos Press
(1981)   *For a Critique of the Political Economy of the Sign,*
          St Louis: Telos Press
(1983)   *In the Shadow of the Silent Majorities,*
          New York: Semiotext(e)
(1987)   *Forget Foucault,*
          New York: Semiotext(e)
(1988)   *America,*
          London: Verso
(1988)   *The Ecstasy of Communication,*
          New York: Semiotext(e)
(1990)   *Seduction,*
          London: Macmillan
(1990)   *Cool Memories I,*
          London: Verso
(1990)   *Fatal Strategies,*
          New York: Semiotext(e)
(1993)   *The Transparency of Evil,*
          London: Verso
(1993)   *Symbolic Exchange and Death,*
          London: Sage Publications
(1994)   *Simulacra and Simulation,*
          University of Michigan
(1994)   *The Illusion of the End,*
          Cambridge: Polity Press
(1995)   *The Gulf War Did Not Take Place,*
          Sydney: Power Publications

Acknowledgements

Chris would like to thank:
Jean Baudrillard, Toby Clark, Cristina Mateo, Corinne Thomas, Libération
and John Dutton.

Zoran is grateful to Mila & Michel in Paris, Maura, Spira and everybody who
had patience, while he ignored them during the work on this book . . .

Biographies

Chris Horrocks trained as a fine artist at Bath Academy, then studied Cultural
History at the Royal College of Art, London. He is currently Senior Lecturer in
Art History at Kingston University, Surrey. He is also the author of *Introducing
Foucault.*

Zoran Jevtic is an illustrator and multimedia author, currently involved in
computer animation, design and music projects. He is also the illustrator
of *Introducing Foucault.*

Index